THE MONASTIC ESTATE

Peter Clery

GUY'S HEAD BOOKS

2015

Published by
GUY'S HEAD BOOKS

2nd Edition 2022
Guy's Head Books
peterclery1@gmail.com

ISBN 978-0-9927266-3-8

For further copies of this book and other books by the same author:

Green Gold -1000 Years of English Land,
The Wealth & Estates of Glastonbury Abbey and
Feeding The Nation: A Celebration of Lincolnshire Farming.

contact: peterclery1@gmail.com

How it all Began

St Benedict, who was a young lad in Italy around A.D. 500, found his friends so debauched that he went to live in a cave, collected followers and ended up founding one of the largest landowning groups ever known in Europe with some two million acres in England alone. The Benedictines - The Black Monks.

Later to start were the **Cistercians**. The order was founded at Citeaux near Dijon in 1098 by a Dorset man, Stephen Harding. The Spirituality which inspired the Order came from **St Bernard of Clairvaux**. Just in England, the White Monks had half a million acres and built monasteries like Fountains, Rievaulx and Byland. Another major order were the **Augustinian Canons** named after St Augustine of Hippo with ¾ million acres in England.

How it all Ended in England

Henry VIII needed money for his extravagances. A survey in 1535 showed just how rich the monasteries were. Henry and his Whitehall advisers wanted this wealth and were not fussy how they got it. Hanging and dismembering a few abbots encouraged the rest of the 'religious' to leave quietly with pensions. Thus King Henry VIII got one sixth of the good land of England with little effort and the wealth and patronage that came with it.

The dirty work was done by **Thomas Cromwell**. Probably no man rose faster and fell more rapidly in all English political history. The son of a Putney smith, after a raffish start in life he joined Cardinal Wolsey's staff and became, in the late 1530's, the most powerful man in the land after the King. But in spite of his massive administrative talents, put to use in the monastic dissolution and much else, he fell foul of the King over the proposed marriage to Anne of Cleves. Jealous nobles saw to his eclipse, a botched execution on 28 July 1540.

Contents

GLASTONBURY
THE BIGGEST MONASTERY IN BRITAIN

1 & 2 *Glastonbury before the dissolution was the largest church in Britain and far the most valuable. It was supported by an estate of 130,000 acres. Nasty work ensured that the abbot was cruelly killed on 15 November 1539 on a trumped up charge of treason. The abbey lands and treasures – gold, silver and precious stones – then went straight to King Henry VIII. The photograph of the ruin today is taken from the east end (the left side of the building above) looking west to the Lady Chapel.*

Acknowledgements

There are many people past and present to whom I owe a major debt of gratitude in respect of material for this book. The main authors consulted appear in the bibliography. To Dr Peter Cunich and Dr Martin Heale, I owe especial thanks. The staff of the Yorkshire Archaeological Society have been particularly helpful in matters pertaining to that county. My cousin Margaret McGregor (willtranscribe@aol.com) has helped greatly with Tudor Latin translations and acknowledgements to Judith Herrin's Miscellany for guidance on medieval sheep farming. Other acknowledgements have been placed in the text. However, the responsibility for my use or misuse of published or other material lies entirely with me.

For illustrations, I am pleased to acknowledge the practical help received from Adam Carruthers (PrintExcel) and for the illustrations, particularly Derry Brabbs, derry.brabbs@virgin.net pp.11, 36, 40, 48, 59, 72-3 and the front cover; Jean Steeds, and Bridgeman Library, p.vi; Sam Brice sbrice@dpas.co.uk p.2; Trinity College, Cambridge, p.9; British Library, p.20; David Ross www.britainexpress.com p.53; Peterborough, St Albans and Ely Cathedral staff, and my apologies for any inadvertent omissions.

Finally, most grateful thanks to my wife Elizabeth for keeping me sane on the IT front and much else besides.

PETER CLERY 2015

I AM GRATEFUL TO READERS OF THE FIRST EDITION WHO HAVE SUGGESTED CERTAIN CHANGES. THESE HAVE BEEN INCORPORATED WHERE APPROPRIATE.

PETER CLERY 2022

NOTE

Throughout this book, the old imperial currency of £ s d has been used as conversion to decimal would not add clarity to the text. For younger readers not familiar with the old currency, 1d=0.42p. 12d = 1shilling.

20 shillings = £1 and 240d = £1.

1 acre = 0.405 ha.

1 ha = 2.471 acres.

The Monastic Estate

Over hundreds of years, the monks and nuns accumulated some four million acres of good English land. A needy, greedy King Henry VIII took the lot – the biggest land grab since the Norman Conquest.

With Thomas Crumwell to do the dirty work.

Not a misprint. This was how he signed himself but the modern spelling is used in this book.

Much is known about the buildings and lives of the monks and nuns. However, almost the whole monastic concept was dependant on the agricultural income from the acres owned by the monasteries. It was this land which King Henry VIII wished to get control of for the sake of the revenues it produced. Whatever the official reasons for the Dissolution of the Monasteries in 1536-40, 'sinful and debauched living' often being given as the excuse, there is little doubt that once the King and his Whitehall advisers, particularly Thomas Cromwell, got an idea of the extent of monastic wealth, they wanted the land and the money it earned. They were not over scrupulous how they got it. Hanging and dismembering a few abbots helped. Money for wars, marriages, divorces and palaces was the priority but schools, colleges and new cathedral foundations did get a look in.

What was the monastic estate? How was it built up? What proportion of England did the monks own? How was it run? Were the 'religious', on balance, fornicating idlers living off the fat of the land or were they charitable and pious men and women giving their lives to study, contemplation, prayers for the departed and doles for the poor? How and why did it all end? Who got the land? Why have we still got wonderful monastic cathedrals like Durham, Ely, Peterborough and Worcester while some of the grandest such as Glastonbury, Reading and Bury St Edmunds are just ruins? This book gives answers.

I

What was the
Monastic Estate?

Number of Houses, monks and nuns. Where the information comes from. Description of the Valor Ecclesiasticus from which much of the material in this book stems. Non-monastic church interests.

In total, 'the religious' probably controlled **some four million acres**, say 16 per cent of the productive land of England and 12 per cent of the total land area. The monastic estate was equal to the total of Bedfordshire, Derbyshire, Leicestershire, Northamptonshire, Nottinghamshire, Rutland, Staffordshire, and Warwickshire added together. There were some 10,000 monks and nuns in 1530 reducing to some 7,000 by the Dissolution. Nuns represented a little less than a fifth of the 'religious' with less than one tenth of the land. But many times this number of lay people were involved. They worked on the farms and at other related activities such as milling, brewing, baking, fulling and tanning but most would have jobs regardless of who owned the land. However, personal servants would have lost their jobs and there were many more of these than of the 'religious' themselves.

Each of the 'religious' therefore controlled, jointly with colleagues, the earning power of an average of at least 400 acres apiece. More than enough for modest living and generous charity. But grand living and property maintenance mopped up most of the money. An abbot of a large House often travelled with a retinue of 20 men and horses, treating himself and being treated as a landed aristocrat although he had a tenure only as long as he held the position of abbot.

There were some 550 Houses of note at the Dissolution which was concluded in a very short time span, effectively 1536-1540, but there were small chantries and cells which survived longer. The monastic assets were very fully documented in the Valor Ecclesiasticus (see below) and it is on Prof. A. Savine's 1909 analysis of this record that much of this book is based. The regular church, which probably owned more land than the monasteries, was not included in the Valor.

For centuries, tax on monastic revenues had been due to the Pope in Rome but these imposts were repatriated from Rome in the early 1530s and therefore due to the English Crown. In those days anyway it was possible to claw back powers from continental authorities. The new English tax was fixed at a tenth of the net income of the English church, more than the Pope had taken. But how much money was due? The last measure of clerical taxation had been in 1291, by Pope Nicholas IV.

Henry VIII and his advisers, initially Cardinal Wolsey but chiefly Thomas Cromwell, wanted to be sure they were getting their due from the monastic estate. Tax evasion was thought to be rife and the thought was often justified. (Glastonbury monks even noted what they did pay against what they should have paid.) A full survey of all

3 *Tisbury Barn, Wiltshire. The Benedictine nuns of Shaftesbury built the longest monastic barn in England. Strictly speaking it was not a 'tithe' barn as it seems to have been used to store produce from their estimated 40,000 acres. (See also p.49.)*

monastic property was therefore ordered. Instructions were given to authorities in every county (trusted gentry and bishops) on 30 January 1535 to carry out this survey and report back by *octabis trinitalis* the same year. Amazingly, and with only very few exceptions, the work was done with a very high degree of accuracy. Intelligent, knowledgeable men on horseback achieved more, it would seem, than would be likely under today's committee dominated, computerised, legalistic environment.

The result was the **Valor**, listing every House by gross income, net income, gross temporal income and net temporal income. Gross and net income included the mis-named Spiritual income, profits from churches and tithes. Temporal income arose from owned property, almost entirely agricultural land and woods though major houses did have urban and trade investments. The data provided was almost entirely in money terms. Acres were hardly ever mentioned. How then to arrive at an idea of how much land was comprised in the monastic estate? There are many records of rents at the time from random sources and one particular record of the rents and 130,000 acres of Glastonbury, carried out in 1516 and translated for the author.

Just as the government today provides an estimate of average farm rents in England, so it has been possible, subject to a wide margin of error, to do the same for 1535-40. This figure has been estimated at 6.5d/acre (2.7p) – higher for fertile, flat land especially permanent pasture and lower for unproductive waste and hill land. It is the relationship between gross temporal income and average rents that has given rise to most of the following estimates of acreages allocated to the monastic orders and their individual Houses. At best, apart from Glastonbury, they can only be approximate. Woods, tracks, waste, ditches and dykes are included as they would be on any estate today.

> By using estimates of acres, it should be possible to bring more meaning to the monastic estate than is possible with Tudor money values. The acreage estimates are subject to a wide margin of error. However …
> It is better to be approximately right than precisely wrong. Attr. J.M.Keynes

2

How the Estate was Built Up

It was on the credulity of lay magnates and sovereigns as to the ability of the monks and nuns to intercede with the Almighty. The donors often had plenty to atone for and it was the job of the 'religious' to organise the salvation of those too busy on earth to do it for themselves. A generous gift of land was seen as the best way of arranging and ensuring this outcome.

It all started with an obscure Italian monk around AD 500. Whilst he did not plan it that way, he inspired the development of enormous landowning corporations in Western Europe influencing thereby scholarship, the arts, architecture and great financial and ecclesiastical patronage, as well as encouraging what seems an unnatural way of living. His celibate followers, in a credulous age, believed that they could speed souls out of purgatory into somewhere more comfortable by interceding on their behalf with the Almighty. Plentiful and regular prayers might even shorten the time spent in hell or so it was suggested to rich noblemen with lots of land and much on their conscience. It was this belief which led to the gifts of great estates to the monasteries all over Europe including England. The credulity tailed off around the end of the 14th century or shortly after. Gifts then also tailed off.

Was this the biggest confidence trick over a millennium or, if both parties believed in it, was it a legitimate form of insurance against the hazards of the next world? Either way, the whole idea came to an inglorious end in England when Henry VIII decided that his interests would best be served by nationalising all the religious houses and had Thomas Cromwell (signing himself Crumwell) to do it for him as Vicar General. Cromwell made a very good job of this. His reward was to be accused of treason and executed.

The Life of St Benedict (our Italian monk) was produced by Pope Gregory the Great in 594 and outlined his concern at the debauchery of his fellow students at Rome. As a result, he went to live in a cave, collected disciples and formulated his Rule under which, initially, not only the Benedictines lived but in modified form most of the other monastic orders which grew up over the years. What is thought to be the earliest copy of The Rule, dated around 750, is in the Bodleian Library, Oxford.

The Rule stressed obedience, humility, abstinence from most nice things including drink, conversation and sex, a self-denying ordinance and a daily and nightly round of prayer. Such religious zeal impressed the laity who, at the outset, certainly held the monks in respect if not awe. However, Benedict over estimated human capacity to abide by such a strict, single gender, un-natural lifestyle. Monastic standards inevitably slipped over the centuries and so did the respect for the monks but not before millions of acres were in monastic hands. Whilst, admittedly, a lot can change in a thousand years, St Benedict would have been distressed to know how far some of his alleged followers had fallen from his ideal. Living in grand abbeys, convents and priories whilst usually ignoring the plight of the poor was not what he intended for his followers. The Venerable Bede felt the same way in 734 (see page 7).

In England, there are many records of gifts, with or without strings, in Anglo-Saxon times. Most of these foundations were easy prey for Danish raiders and violently destroyed. Some at least were restored after the Norman Conquest as King William I undoubtedly wanted to keep the Church on side as long as it was on his side. Installing French abbots and monks in all the abbeys and major priories (with the exception of Worcester and Saxon Bishop Wulfstan) ensured the loyalty of the monastic interest. The **Glastonbury** cartularies have numerous examples of pre-Conquest gifts to the abbey. Three will suffice to give a flavour of the transactions: in 970 at Idmiston, Wiltshire, King Edgar granted ten measures to widow Elfswyt who became a nun and endowed the abbey with this land; in 663 King Ine of Wessex granted ten measures of land to Haemgils, Abbot of Glastonbury, and at Baltonsborough in 744 Lulla, handmaid of Christ granted to Abbot Tunberht and the monks of Glastonbury ten measures of land … putting the charter on the altar of St Peter and Paul with her own hand. In this piecemeal way, the largest monastic land holding in England was built up to 130,000 acres.

By contrast, **Peterborough** went for the big stuff. It was endowed by one of the largest documented land grants to any monastery. In 653, Abbot Seaxwulf of Peterborough (then Medeshamstede) received from King Wulfhere of Mercia land on the following terms as described in the Anglo–Saxon (Laud) Chronicle thus:

> The king, standing before all his thanes, spoke in a loud voice: 'Thanks be to the high almighty God … I Wulfhere freely give to the abbot and monks of the monastery these lands, waters, meres, fens, weirs and all the land situated thereabouts and which belong to my kingdom so that no man shall have any authority but the abbot and monks. This is the gift'.

There follows a detailed description of a perambulation involving many names and places which can be identified today. The peroration ends:

> 'This is but a small benefaction but I desire that they shall hold it so royally and freely that no tax or rent may be taken.'

The gift appears to include most if not all of the land within a ten-mile radius of the abbey and could have been as much as 100,000 acres. If that was a small benefaction what would have been a large one?

In this way and through thousands of endowments and bequests, the great monastic estate in England was built up. The monks were expected to work out the salvation of those wealthy donor/magnates too busy to do this for themselves. However, strings were attached to many gifts. Apart from prayers for their own souls as well as their relations, the donors often required corrodians (assured places for board and lodging) in the House for relations, friends and even servants. Annuities sometimes had to be paid and compulsory charities performed. These liabilities accounted for the difference between gross and net income as shown in the Valor Ecclesiasticus.

In general, but there are certainly examples to contradict this, the abbeys, convents and priories held on to what land they had in the 13th and 14th centuries right

Give me a good digestion, Lord,
And also something to digest
Give me a healthy body, Lord,
With sense to keep it at its best.

Give me a healthy mind, O Lord,
To keep the good and pure in sight
Which seeing wrong is not appalled
But finds a way to put it right.

Give me a mind that is not bored,
That does not whimper,
whine or sigh.
Don't let me worry overmuch,
About that fussy thing called 'I'.

Give me a sense of humour, Lord,
Give me the grace to see a joke,
To get some happiness from life
And pass it on to other folk.

4   *A monk's prayer reputedly from Glastonbury Abbey. (The abbey and Black Designs.)*

through to the Dissolution. They did not sell land (though exchanges were arranged) and generally did not have free funds to buy more land (the Statute of Mortmain forbade this or discouraged it by heavy fines) and gifts dried up. Abbot Whyting of Glastonbury, in a forlorn attempt at bribing Thomas Cromwell with the gift of the advowson (the profitable power to appoint a priest) of West Monkton church stated that,

> in trewth this was the first granted out of the monastery as far as I can find knowledge.

There were, as outlined above, many monastic settlements in England before the Conquest but they fell into two conflicting groups: the more easy going Irish /Celtic Houses and those following the new, stricter Benedictine rule. The Synod of Whitby was convened in 664 to resolve these differences. The Benedictines won and the Celtic houses faded away without leaving a noticeable land legacy for the Benedictines to inherit.

One of the more unusual arrivals on the landowning scene were the Knights Templar and Knights Hospitaller. In 1185, less than 25 years before their downfall, Geoffrey Fitz Stephen, the Grand Master of the English Templar Preceptories (described as a princely figure with artistic tastes – not cut out for a military career?), initiated an Inquisition* of all Templar land in England.

The Order had a presence in all English counties except Norfolk, Cheshire, Lancashire, Cumbria, Durham and Northumberland. No indication of the full extent of their landholding was found. However, in Kent alone, where their presence was very light, they had over 1,000 acres of arable which could be increased by 50 per cent for meadow, pasture and woodland. The average rent was around 6d/acre (no labour services noted) but Hamo de Chilham paid £2 18s 8d – 10d/acre – for 58 acres of arable, three acres of meadow, and 13 acres of wood. In Lincolnshire, the total Templar holding was put at 96 carucates of arable plus meadow, pasture and wood along with 344 tofts (a dwelling, buildings, gardens and grass paddock) for the villein/peasant families. If a carucate was 160 acres (in Lincolnshire) and half of the arable area allowed for meadow, pasture and woods and a toft put at 10-12 acres, then the Templar holding in Lincolnshire alone would have been up to some 25,000 acres.

*Information from the Inquisition translated by Beatrice Lees.

3
WHO WERE THE MONKS WITH ALL THE MONEY?

The **Benedictines** were the largest (in numbers) and wealthiest Order. They held about two million acres – half of the estimated monastic total and 48 per cent of the £136,000 monastic net income. If, and it is a big if, agriculture was half of the gross national product in 1535 and the monks had 16 per cent of the productive land, then the Benedictines controlled 8 per cent of the economy. Known as the black monks from the colour of their cowled habits, they established 280 monasteries and 90 nunneries in Britain with a deserved reputation for high living in the larger Houses but no obvious record of helping their poorer brethren. They were leaders in agricultural and estate management in the 12th and 13th centuries in addition to their scholarship in the cloister and scriptorium. The excellent farming activities of Prior Henry of Eastry at Canterbury are considered in Chapter 5 and under the county of Kent. The first post-Conquest Benedictine foundation was Battle Abbey in Sussex in 1087. After a prod from the Pope, it was commissioned as a war memorial by William the Conqueror. (See County of Sussex.) William evicted most monastic and secular clergy from the Saxon houses installing, as he saw it, go-ahead ambitious mainly Benedictine French bishops and abbots, his friends and relations from Normandy.

From this time, the foundations were laid of the great landed monastic estates and by the Dissolution, 9 out of 10 of the wealthiest religious Houses, by net income, were Benedictine. The other House in the top ten was Syon, the wealthy **Bridgettine** nuns at Twickenham. The order in respect of gross temporal income, which reflected almost entirely land, was somewhat different and is set out in Chapter 4.

From the outset of monasticism, trouble was foreseen. The vows of chastity, poverty, obedience as well as silence often became more than flesh and blood could adhere to, especially when the necessities for high living were so amply to hand. Apart from home brewed beer, cart loads of beef, mutton, pork, bacon, poultry, eggs, fish, malt, wine, spices, condiments and all sorts of provender were being regularly shipped in to the rich houses from the 13th century onwards and religious observance and charity seemed to have suffered a parallel decline. All this was foreseen in AD 734 and warned against by the Venerable Bede, himself a Benedictine monk. Writing from his little cell in Jarrow priory to Bishop Egbert of York, of whom he suspected shortcomings, he cautioned against the collection of assets in the name of monasticism for personal pride or gain by those who failed to understand or carry through the monastic tradition implicit in St Benedict's rules.

> It is your duty, I say, to ensure that in those places that are consecrated to God, the devil does not set up his kingdom in case conflict replaces peace, discord piety, drunkenness sobriety and fornication and murder take the throne of chastity and charity.

The very sins which 800 years later gave Henry VIII the excuse to take the land and demolish the monasteries. Bede went on to warn that those who failed in their duties would be thrown into outer darkness where there will be weeping and gnashing of teeth and he advised the holy father to avoid all idle chatting and gossiping and other evils of the unrestrained tongue. Not advice which would be welcome to mobile phone operators today. Bede thought that all non-essential monastic endowments should be returned to the donors. Had his advice been followed, there would have been no monastic estate to excite Henry VIII.

Groups of pious men and women watched with dismay the slackening of the Benedictine cult and sought to do better.

As Canons (not monks), the **Augustinians** had a broader outlook on life than the Benedictines. They did not have the same reputation as the Cistercians for agricultural innovation but were in fact the second biggest landowners with over three quarters of a million acres. They were allowed out to take services in churches affiliated to their House and could move more freely in their local communities than the Benedictines or Cistercians. Wealthy landowners with statutory religious responsibilities found them useful as they could undertake such church duties. Endowments could and did follow. They wore a black habit with a white surplice and were known as **Black Canons**. There were some 170 monasteries and 23 nunneries and all professed, in theory anyway, to adhere to the Rule of St Augustine, slightly easier than that of Benedict. They had something of a reputation for financing hospitals. Their largest estates were Cirencester, Waltham Holy Cross in Essex (the last House to go down in the country), Merton in Surrey, Leicester St Mary and St Osyth in Essex. As an Order, it seems that they put at least some of their income to good use, like founding hospitals.

Initially, the **Cistercians** did do better than the Benedictines in terms of religious observance. Known as the **White Monks** because of their obvious white habits, they were founded in France in 1109, by an Englishman from Dorset, Stephen Harding, and reported to the Mother House of Citeaux. From there, St Bernard of Clairvaux provided the spiritual input. Some 80 monasteries and 30 nunneries were established in England with about half a million acres – about 12 per cent of the monastic estate and wealth. They were initially austere in their lives and severe in their discipline. They favoured out of the way bleak locations for their monasteries. Croxden, Fountains, Furness, Jervaulx and Rievaulx are examples but land was an asset in ample supply as far as Norman magnates were concerned. They had more than they knew what to do with. Even an apparently generous gift of a thousand acres meant little to them if their souls were regularly prayed for, places found in convents for their womenfolk when necessary and bleak or derelict land was brought into production, thus enhancing the value of their surrounding property. The Cistercians were very good at this in their early years. Working much in the north, they could organise their land there free of the hindrances of the manorial open field strip system still common in the Midlands.

However there were mixed feelings even then about such activities. **Walter Map**, a 12th-century secular, cynical cleric, said of the Cistercians that

> they obtain from a rich man a valueless and despised plot in the heart of a great wood by much feigning of innocence and long importunity, putting in God at every other word. The wood is cut down, stubbed up and levelled into a plain. Bushes give way to barley, willows to wheat, withies to vines and it may be that to give them full time for these operations their prayers have to be somewhat shortened.

5 *A very early, boastful 'selfie' from a Canterbury monk. 'Scriptor: (Eadwine) I am the chief of scribes and neither my praise nor my fame shall die. Shout out, oh my letter, who I may be'. 'Letter: By its fame your script proclaims you, Eadwine who the painted figure shows, alive through the ages whose genius the beauty of this book proclaims'. Eadwine, with a goose quill in his right hand, might be copying a rent roll but more likely a valued psalter.*

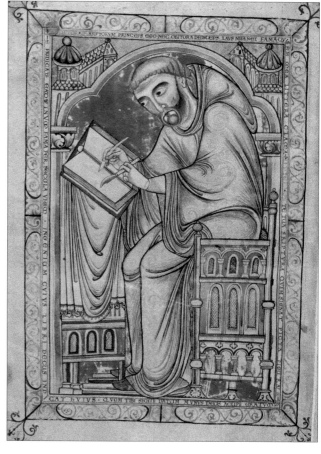

But on balance such activities must have been to the common good. Stubbing out tree roots before the days of the JCB would have been hard work but, given time, rooting pigs would have helped a lot.

The Cistercians evolved a system of second-class lay brothers to do the hard graft of land clearance and day-to-day farming on a very large scale on estates (granges) extending well beyond the guidance that all properties should be within a day's walk of the Mother House. This left the refined choir monks to get on with reading, writing, praying and chanting without getting their hands dirty. But the abbots, priors and abbesses still had final responsibility for their estates and therefore needed to acquire or have on hand land agency skills if the House was to prosper. For a while this worked very well and the money rolled in from farming skills and innovation. They were good at growing cereals as well as dairy farming to produce butter and cheese. But wool was the best cash crop up to the mid-14th century though serious outbreaks of sheep scab in 1280-90 caused major disruption and financial loss from the inability to fulfill forward contracts unwisely entered into.

Based on 200 fleeces per sack, **Fountains** had at least 15,000 sheep, **Rievaulx** 12,000 and **Jervaulx** 10,000, all Yorkshire Cistercian monasteries. However, some of this wool may have been bought in as the monks did become dealers in wool as well as producers, an activity certainly outside the spirit of the founder's intentions.

The lay brothers became steadily disenchanted with their hard work and inferior status. (Shearing time must have been a daunting business with just hand clippers.) Also, the hours will have taken a toll of their working abilities. They were rarely excused the daily round of prayer : 2am for Vigils and Matins, 4am for Lauds, 6am for Prime, 10am for Tierce, 12 noon for Sext, 3pm Nones, 6pm Vespers and 8pm Compline. If they stuck to this schedule, with barely five hours' sleep, it is a mystery how they ever got much outside work done. They were only allowed in the nave of the church and a segregated dormitory was always built for them with separate eating and toilet arrangements. This set-up did not seem very much in line with Christ's teachings, even those parts of which the lay brothers were allowed to know about. Out on the granges, away from the beady eyes of the senior bosses, things were rather better for the lay brothers – they organised matters that way and Head Office benefited financially.

However an 'Act of God', if the plague can be so called, put an effective end to the lay-brother system. The Black Death in 1348, with subsequent outbreaks, took a terrible toll of lives and the remaining choir monks took to letting their estates where they could and only kept on such granges for which they could find staff. Great areas of Cistercian monasteries therefore were un-occupied where lay brothers once ate and slept. Decadence insidiously crept in and soon the Cistercians like the Benedictines were little more than landlords of great swathes of rural land, living very well off the proceeds – just what Bede had warned against. Have sundry abbots ended up in outer darkness wailing and weeping and gnashing their teeth? If not, why not? Where is the justice?

The **Canons of the Premonstratensian Order,** also known as Norbertines after their founder St Norbert, generally sought to follow Cistercian guidelines and wore similar white robes and were known as White Canons. They answered initially to the Mother House at Premontre in France. Their first English House was at **Newsham**, west of Grimsby, Lincolnshire, established in 1143. This was a little foundation which never grew beyond some 2,500 acres. Like the Augustinians, they were not, strictly speaking, monks but canons who involved themselves in extra-curricular activities outside the monastic walls. At the finish, they had 34 monasteries and four nunneries, about 130,000 acres and were fourth in the landowning hierarchy.

The **Cluniac Order** was founded in France in 910 by the Duke of Aquitaine and the English Houses, of which there were 32, were all subject to the authority of the Abbot of Cluny. The monks wore black habits and generally did their best to abide by St Benedict's rules. The best known English Houses were **Lewes** in Sussex, **Castle Acre** in Norfolk, **Thetford** in Suffolk and **Wenlock** in Shropshire but there were a number of small 'cells' which failed to make the grade and faded away. Being directly under the control of the Abbot of Cluny in France, Cluniacs were in difficulties when England and France were at war, being regarded as Alien Houses. They wished to be free of this control and come under English jurisdiction. They ultimately succeeded in 1404 but not before the Abbot of Cluny and his advisers called the idea *una magna fatuitas*. Shades of the Brussels bureaucrats' attitude to the UK leaving the EU? At the Dissolution, the Cluniacs had about 100,000 acres, fifth in the league of landed wealth.

The Charterhouse monks, **Carthusians**, came closest to sticking with St Benedict. Their life involved living alone, having food brought anonymously through a hatch

6 & 7 *Mount Grace, a Carthusian charterhouse priory, north of Thirsk, Yorkshire. The church was the only place where the hermit-like monks met, being allowed out just for the services. Their individual mini-cottage cells were, however, commodious. The doorways to four of the five units are shown in the picture below, on the west side of the enormous cloister green. All was not always sweetness and light in Carthusian Houses. In the south-west corner of the cloister was the prison, used to incarcerate re-captured runaway monks and those who 'lacked discipline'. (See also p.73.)*

and meeting colleagues only briefly for church services. They were said to espouse hair shirts and generally coarse clothing. However, it seemed that, at the beginning of the 16th century, they were the only order with a waiting list to join. How so? The answer could be found at **Mount Grace** in Yorkshire. There, a typical monk's cell has been reconstructed. Cell is hardly the right word. The ground floor comprises study room with fireplace, bedroom, enclosed veranda looking over small, neat garden, covered walk way to private toilet emptied daily by others and, upstairs, a large airy workroom for such activities as weaving. Given that lot and undisturbed peace and quiet, it is not surprising that there was a waiting list. One suspects there would be a waiting list today (apart from the hair shirts) as in fact there seems to be for a residual Carthusian House at Parkminster, Cowfold, in West Sussex. This is a unique survival from medieval times but probably without quite so strict a regime as was originally imposed.

The Order was neither very wealth nor very large – there were ten monasteries (no nunneries) in England reporting directly to the Pope until Henry VII intervened. In all they probably had perhaps 60,000 acres and an urban presence and assets. Their net income was some £2,958 – just over two per cent of the monastic total. **Sheen** in Surrey founded by Henry V in 1414 was by far the largest House with a net income of £778. The Order developed in the 15th century as benefactors found their austere regime more relevant to an effort to please the Almighty than that of the increasingly indolent Benedictines. Though urged to reform, the Benedictines resented the rise of the Carthusians and a consequent decline in their own influence (and relative wealth). The Order was originally founded by St Bruno at Chartreuse in France, now better known for the green liqueur of that name. The annual charitable generosity of the Carthusians varied greatly. In 1535 the Coventry Charterhouse managed £77, Sheen £44, London £5 and Mount Grace only 5s.

The **Knights Templar** were founded around 1099 by Cistercian Bernard of Clairvaux as a military order of monks. Their purpose was to fight to regain and protect the Holy Places of the Christian religion in Jerusalem from the Arabs and latterly the Turks – the 'Saracens'. This led to the, less than successful, Crusades. The military strength of the Order was considerably weakened by an unsuccessful invasion of Syria in 1291 and the near obliteration of their forces in 1302.

Originally termed the Poor Fellow-Soldiers of Christ, the name rapidly became obsolete as the Order grew in wealth and power acting as political agents and bankers as well as soldiers. The Templar tag came from an alternative name for the order – Knights of the Temple of Solomon in Jerusalem. When the Knights refused to lend more money to King Philip of France who already owed them considerable sums, the Order was forcibly disbanded in 1308 amid accusations of heresy and homosexuality. These were admitted under torture but later rescinded, leading to a worse death for many at the stake.

Two morals here: Do not meddle in Middle Eastern affairs unless you have the power, might and intention to see the matter through and do not lend money to despots with more power than you have.

In England, the Knights were generously funded with land by King Stephen, Queen Matilda as Countess of Boulogne and King Richard I, the Crusader. He would probably have been more use to the nation looking to his own kingdom instead of pursuing military adventures in the eastern Mediterranean, getting captured and having to be bailed out with a massive ransom raised in taxes from the whole country. The Cistercians and other Houses had to contribute a whole year's wool clip, their main source of revenue.

The Templars centralised all their rents and profits from their English estates in London, the money then being directed to the Holy War effort. Their first London base was the **Old Temple** in Holborn and latterly the **New Temple** between Fleet Street and the Thames, described then as a Grand Palace but now mainly remembered as a station on the District and Circle lines on the underground and a home for lawyers. The Old Temple at Holborn was sold to the Bishop of Lincoln in the 1160s. The property comprised a round church, various houses on the south side of Holborn, stables and gardens. Big London land deals are not just a recent phenomenon and the Bishop no doubt found the Old Temple to be a useful London base as well as a good investment.

When in 1309-10 the Order was disbanded in England, the great majority of its considerable assets were passed to the more pacific **Hospitallers** though the Crown held on to at least part including the Lordship of Burstwick in Yorkshire.

Apart from on the London underground, the Temple name lives on in many parts of the country – Temple, Templeton and Templecombe in Cornwall, Devon and Somerset and Temple Meads, Bristol's main line station. The Templar Church, Dover, Temple Guiting in Gloucester, Temple Grafton in Warwick and Temple Normanton in Derby. Temple Sowerby is in North Yorkshire but there is nothing to show for Temple Bruer in Lincolnshire, one of the main Templar bases. It was thin un-reclaimed land then but is now growing good crops of barley, wheat and grass for processing. Temple Bruer was in the vicinity of Ashby de la Laund just off the A15 Sleaford to Lincoln road.

The **Valor** records the Hospitallers as having London assets with a net income of £2,081, second only to Benedictine Westminster but they were an Order, not a House and their possessions must not be confused with those of individual Houses. Much of their wealth was thought to be in urban property. If one third was rural, this could represent some 40,000 acres. In addition, in the country, there would appear to have been another 60,000 acres listed separately and based on temporal income. All the land went to the Crown in 1540 but whether it amounted to 100,000 acres has to be a matter for conjecture.

The **Gilbertines** were the only native English House, founded by Gilbert of Sempringham in Lincolnshire in 1131. They were mixed Houses but this did not mean much as the monks and nuns only came together in church on Sunday and were then not allowed to see each other but could share the singing. Strictly, they were canons and canonesses. Gilbert got going in a competitive environment by establishing smaller Houses than the Benedictines or Cistercians allowed and working harder at the farming. Perhaps benefactors also liked the idea of an Order not controlled from across the Channel. *English prayers for English souls.* There were some 16 Houses, 50,000 acres, eighth in the landowning league. Gilbertines generally followed the Augustinian code of conduct. The monks had black habits and a white cloak. The nuns were also in black but with a white cowl. That way they could tell each other from behind if they should accidently meet. Appropriate action could then be taken.

The **Bridgettines**, stemming from a Swedish order honouring St Bridget, were an influential, fashionable and very wealthy Order of nuns with just one House at Syon in Middlesex. Founded as late as 1415 by Henry V, the members of the House came from the cream of female society as well as London merchant families who made the grade socially and financially. There was no scandal and the Abbess with the aid of a confessor and other brethren ran a very tight ship which allowed for a high level of intellectual activity including an excellent library. They probably accumulated up to about 40,000 acres, quite a lot of it in West Sussex. They had a net income of £1,735. Much of their land came from alienated houses when Anglo-French relations were such that confiscation of French assets was the order of the day. In 1404, the Crown took over all revenue from alien (French-owned) Houses but re-distributed quite a lot back to the monasteries and nunneries. St Michael's Mount in Cornwall was a case in point, taken from the Mother House of Mont St Michel and, after a legal dispute with King's College Cambridge, was passed to the Bridgettines.

Among the minor landowning groups were the **Trinitarians** who were founded with the unusual brief of negotiating ransoms for Christians kidnapped by Saracens. Others were the **Bonhommes**, the **Grandmontines**, the **Tironensians**, **Bethlemites** and the **Franciscan** friars. All in all, they probably held little more than 50,000 acres.

4

How much of England did the Nuns and Monks Own?

The figure suggested in the table below is some four million acres or 16 per cent of the productive land. Of the whole country, the proportion was of the order of 12 per cent.

The monastic acres are based on the gross temporal income for each county less a 10 per cent allowance for non-agricultural income. Of this four million total, the nuns had an estimated 380,000 acres, almost 10 per cent. Many convents and nunneries were small with only a few hundred acres: 25 nunneries had little more than a single farm to support them. The exceptions were: Bridgettine Syon, noted above as an Order; Shaftesbury, businesslike Benedictine ladies but financially strapped in relation to their outgoings, with around 38,000 acres; and Benedictine Wilton where the nuns had perhaps 20,000 acres but much of their income taken in kind including wheat, barley, oats, capons, hens, geese, pigeons (800), wool, pepper and eight loads of hay. They only had an income of £10 from their own woods so will have had to spend a lot of money to keep warm.

The ten richest Houses for gross temporal income, closely correlated to landed wealth, were: **Glastonbury** (130,000 acres), **Westminster**, **Canterbury**, **York St Mary**, **Bury St Edmunds**, **Reading**, **Abingdon**, **St Albans**, **Ramsey** and **Peterborough**.

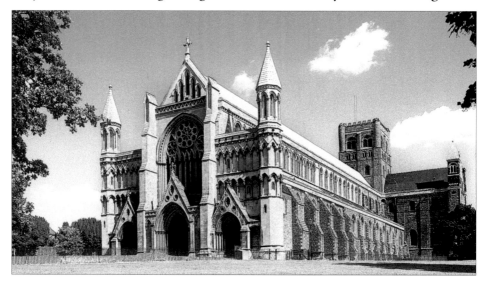

8 *St Albans, a very rich abbey, possibly with 65-70,000 acres, was on the main route north in medieval times. This could account for a report in 1250 that the monastery had stalls for 300 horses (see p.52). Around A.D. 950 Abbot Wulsin indulged in early town planning with a new settlement and market outside the north gate of the abbey.*

Estimate of Monastic Acreages

County	Productive County Acres inc. Woods	Monastic acres	% of county
Bedfordshire	257,000	55000	20%
Berkshire	366,000	144000	39%
Buckinghamshire	401,000	28000	7%
Cambridge	491,000	72000	15%
Cheshire	538,000	50000	9%
Cornwall	605,000	24000	4%
Cumberland	581,000	28000	5%
Derbyshire	496,000	12000	2%
Devon	1,212,000	136000	11%
Dorset	482,000	151000	31%
Durham	440,000	45000	10%
Essex	810,000	209000	26%
Gloucester	661,000	154000	22%
Hampshire	715,000	144000	20%
Hereford	446,000	18000	4%
Hertford	333,000	72000	22%
Huntingdon	208,000	85000	41%
Kent	749,000	178000	24%
Lancashire	822,000	55000	7%
Leicestershire	475,000	71000	15%
Lincolnshire	1,517,000	230000	15%
Middlesex*		200000	
Norfolk	1,070,000	143000	13%
Northampton	560,000	109000	19%
Northumberland	708,000	26000	4%
Nottingham	448,000	53000	12%
Oxfordshire	412,000	76000	18%
Shropshire	720,000	64000	9%
Somerset	857,000	266000	30%
Staffordshire	597,000	58000	10%
Suffolk	764,000	135000	18%
Surrey	282,000	123000	43%
Sussex	668,000	80000	12%
Warwick	496,000	91000	18%
Westmoreland	250,000	3000	1%
Wiltshire	738,000	126000	17%
Worcestershire	402,000	129000	32%
Yorkshire	2,729,000	326000	12%
TOTALS (approx.)	24,400,000	3,970,000	16%

* See next page.

The acreage of 3.97m is almost certainly an understatement as several Houses were not included in Prof. Savine's analysis. These included Netley (Hants), Kingswood (Wilts), Creake (Norfolk), Bayham (Sussex), St Augustine (Bristol), Sawley (Lancs), Easby (Yorks) and Melchbourne (Beds). No estimate has been made of the wealth of these Houses nor of their possible acreages.

County Comments

Six counties had 30 per cent or more in monastic hands. **Berkshire** included Reading and Abingdon, the tenth and twelfth wealthiest Houses and 2,500 Glastonbury acres. **Dorset** had Shaftesbury and Sherborne as major Houses along with 12,000 acres of Glastonbury land.

In **Huntingdon**, Ramsey probably held of the order of 50,000 acres. **Somerset** was dominated by Glastonbury. **Surrey**, a fairly small county, had substantial Houses – Chertsey, Merton and Southwark. **Worcester** was dominated by Evesham and the cathedral.

Yorkshire had the largest number of religious houses (67) and the largest area of monastic land at over 300,000 acres – 12 per cent of the county. The richest House was St Mary's Benedictine Abbey in York. Records are scanty but St Mary's may have held some 70,000 acres plus urban investments though this is very uncertain and the St Mary's position in the monastic wealth hierarchy is correspondingly uncertain. Fountains Abbey, by contrast, had a fairly certain lowland acreage of 20,000 plus 50,000 acres of moorland around Malham Tarn not included in the above figures as such but with an allowance for their very limited productivity.

* **London and Middlesex** present a problem. Two leading Houses and several other substantial Houses had their head offices in London and their estates reported there and were so noted in the Valor. It is not possible to apportion these lands to the counties in which they were situated. The main Houses were Westminster and Syon. (As noted above, the Hospitaller Knights of St John were an Order as were the Bridgettines at Syon.) There were other substantial houses such as St Mary's Graces, St Mary's Bishopsgate, St Helens, the London Charterhouse and the Minories with land in the country outside Middlesex. The single-figure guesstimate is that these London-based Houses had about 200,000 acres reporting to them. This is the figure in the Table but of course it bears no relation to the actual monastic acreage in London and Middlesex. Westminster probably had around 80,000 acres which comprised 110 estates mainly in Essex, Worcester and Middlesex; Syon, around 40,000 acres. The balance comes from estimate of farmland and woods held by the other London Houses and the Hospitaller Knights.

5

Esate Management, Farming, Woods and Wine

Monks as farmers and landlords initially, then farm managers and landlords and finally, basically, just landlords. Demesne and customary land. How the estates were run. Farming outputs.

Not much in the way of farm labour from the monks at any time apart from the very early days. Their role was increasingly that of land managers. Most estates in the Midlands and South came ready-made with a complement of serfs or customary tenants occupying most of the land except the demesne but usually with duties of labour owed to the House. The customary tenants, who made up by far the largest section of the monastic economy in the early years, did not have an easy time. They lived in what now would be regarded as miserable hovels with nothing that would pass for a window. Their daily workload, often on sparse food, is impossible to contemplate today. However, it is possible to imagine some pleasure in their lives, say in late spring with bees at work in their fruit trees, hens starting to lay and cattle and sheep improving in condition after winter hardships with lambs popping out unexpectedly, as they do. There would also be the hope of a good harvest ahead.

At the outset, the demesne was land, often the best, kept in hand with woods and fishings, to supply the immediate needs of the monastery. In some cases, particularly in the North, the monks were given tracts of unused land and encouraged to clear and improve the ground. This applied particularly to the Cistercians in Yorkshire as noted on page 9. The sheep and wool enterprises of not just the Cistercians but of all the main Orders have already been well recorded by others. Suffice to say here that the author is full of admiration for the shepherds – becaria – who looked after thousands of sheep with no more kit than a crook and tar oil salve (against the

maggot fly and scab). Lambing time would have been as essential to profit then as it is now and all the shearing was done just with hand clippers. The records do not mention sheep dogs but these surely would have been vital to managing the large flocks on hill and lowland alike.

On such a simple tool was the woollen wealth of monasteries and all England dependant. A medieval manual has relevance today, 'Each shepherd ought to … enclose and repair the folds … hedges, fences and hurdles … He ought to pasture and feed his sheep well and watch over them so that they are not killed or tormented by dogs, stolen, lost or exchanged and they do not pasture in forbidden moors, ditches and bogs thereby contracting illness … All sheep ought to be marked with the mark of the Lord and no ewe should be milked after the feast of Our Lady (8 September) because they are then slow to mate and … late lambs will be worth less'. So might a competent abbot or prior have instructed his farm staff.

The **Templar Knights** were military men. They did not do land clearance and did not get involved in farming. They were landlords from start to finish. To facilitate management, they followed a policy, where they could, of fixing money rents rather than encouraging boon works (compulsory labour by the servile tenantry). They were succeeded by the Hospitallers. From Rainham, Essex, the most detailed record of a farming lease set up by the Hospitallers on 160 acres of ex-Templar land is set out below. It gives a precise idea of agricultural and legal practice some 700 years ago but there is a modern ring to much of it. The stocking and cropping of the farm comes to life. The lease, for five years for £25 10s. (7.3d/acre), shows a detailed account of the farming as well as the legislation.

> This indenture bears witness that 12 July 7 Edward III [1333] brother Leonard de Tybert Prior of the Hospital of St John of Jerusalem in England granted to Thomas Kempe of Wenyngtone, the manor of the said hospital 'de la More' in the county of Essex with all its appurtenances; to have and to hold with all the profits taken and able to be taken from the feast of the Nativity of St John the Baptist last past until the complete term of 5 years next following; viz. in such a way that the same Thomas shall pay from thence to the aforesaid prior at the clerks' fountain [Clerkenwell] in any one year of the said 5 years £2 10s. sterling … and he is to do and maintain all the other rents and services incumbent on the said manor for the same time, and moreover he is to repair and maintain all the buildings, walls and hedges of the said prior there beyond timber for housbote and heybote and at the end of the said 5 years he is to give back and render to the aforesaid prior or his successors, the aforesaid manor with all its appurtenances in place concerning beasts and other goods in such good state as he received them: viz. with 2 cart-horses each worth 13s 4d, 3 oxen worth 16s per head, one bull and 20 cows worth 13s 4d per head, 6 steers worth 10s per head, 5 calves worth 2s a head, 2 rams, 2 wethers, 133 ewes worth 16d per head and with 26 acres of land sown with wheat, 42 acres of land sown with rye, 14 acres of land sown with winter barley, 12 acres of land sown with beans, 2 acres of land sown with peas, 3 acres of land sown with barley and 6 acres of land sown with oats, one acre of meadow and a half, 40 acres of fallow land, 14 acres of manured land, one cart bound with iron with all the harness for 2 horses worth 15s, 2 ploughs with all their tackle, 2 harrows.
>
> To which payments, repairs and surrender, faithfully to be performed, the same Thomas obliges himself his heirs and executors
>
> **Margaret McGregor**

The peak of monastic farming occurred in the early 14th century, the time of '**High Farming**'. The activities of Benedictine **Peterborough** abbey give a flavour of how it and most of the large Houses would have been involved. Peterborough ran a herd of over 1,200 **cattle** and a fluctuating flock of up to 9,000 **sheep**. Management was centralised and sophisticated with birth and mortality rates calculated. The fertility rates for cows were 86 per cent. Grazing was seasonally apportioned over the abbey's 23 manors in demesne, most of which seem to have been within King Wulfhere's gift. The cattle herd produced beef, tallow, hides, milk, butter, cheese and draft power. Dairy products and draft oxen were the most important elements. Milk yields were around 100-150 gallons (600-700 litres) per year; 1,000 gallons is now commonplace. From the sheep flock, wool, meat and skins (parchment and clothing) were the major items with wool by far the most important. Sales of livestock and livestock products were a major source of money for the Peterborough Abbey Building Fund, money put to particularly good effect on the west front.

9 *Ploughing.*

10 *Sowing.*

11 *Harrowing. Walter of Henley advised, in 1322, proper harrowing in of seed 'or els crows and other byrdes will eate and bear away the cornes'.*

12 *Harvesting.*

13 *Carting.*

From the Luttrell Psalter c.1320. Sir Geoffrey Luttrell was a wealthy Lincolnshire landowner who commissioned his own 'hymn book'.

A guess at stocking rates suggests that the grazing animals may have taken up 10-15,000 acres. Arable demesne would have come on top of this for which the **oxen** would be essential. There may well have been 2-3,000 oxen equal to, say, 300 eight-ox gangs which at 15-20 acres to a gang suggests 5-6,000 acres arable worked by ox power. The Peterborough monks were ahead of the game in substituting **horses** for oxen. In the 12th century, they had one horse per 40 oxen. By the early 14th century, they were up to 16 horse for 40 oxen. But the national average was about half this. The monks also ran a stud farm for both riding and draught horses. Half the oats grown went to the horses.

Pigs were important as a source of pork, bacon and lard for the monastic household providing half the requirement for the 140 mouths to be fed. The account rolls again show a high degree of management. Walter of Henley stated (*c.*1280) that a sow ought to bear twice a year and, at each farrowing, she ought to bear at least seven pigs. Peterborough monks easily achieved this and such figure had hardly been improved on in the 20th century. Peas and beans played a larger part in pig rations than today. Even the pigs on the Cottingham manor in Rockingham forest relied mainly on cereals, peas and beans for their feed. The traditional idea of pigs rooting around in the forest and living on not much else was set out by Seneschaucy, an anonymous writer on estate management around 1276.

> A swineherd ought to be on those manors where pigs can support themselves and find their own food without help from the grange in forest, wood, marsh, waste … If there are no woods, marsh or waste where pigs could support themselves without having to be kept entirely on food from the grange no swineherd ought to be employed and only as many pigs be kept on such manors as can be fed in August on the stubble and the leavings of the grange when corn for sale is being threshed.

This negative attitude certainly did not apply to the pig units of Peterborough abbey.

Poultry were useful. Hens, roosters, capons, pigeons, geese, ducks, swans, pheasants, chicks and eggs were all documented in the accounts. Most of the chicken and eggs came as rents in kind from the tied, customary tenantry. They supplied sufficient for each of the 60 monks to have eggs three times a week for much of the year. However, abbey staff herded 600-800 geese a year on the stubbles – hatching these would have been a major task. There was also enough dovecote capacity to provide 1,500-2,500 pigeons, no doubt fed mostly at the expense of the tenants' crops. The developed and organised farming demonstrated by these monastic accounts is far removed from the idea of medieval agricultural inefficiency but skills and techniques were involved which were not easily available to the customary tenants.

Original sources: Fitzwilliam Account Rolls 2388, 233 2389 – 'Pastoral Husbandry on a Medieval Estate' by Kathleen Biddick.

Another Benedictine House with a high reputation for husbandry was **Canterbury** under Prior Henry of Eastry, also described under the County notes for Kent (page 54). Prior Henry ran some 14,000 sheep for wool, dairy and meat as well as extensive cattle herds for ox power, meat and dairying on the Priory's Kentish estates. Nor were arable crops neglected. He understood the value of legumes leaving more fertile ground behind (nitrates fixed by plant roots). Peas and beans were grown as were vetches on land he reclaimed on Romney marsh. **Winchester**, along with other major Houses, was involved in high farming in much the same way as Peterborough.

But farming profits declined in the 14th and 15th centuries and the Black Death made terrible inroads into the labour force. As a result, the big Houses steadily moved to letting their land. This lessened the risk of loss and greatly decreased the need for skilled experienced 'hands on' farm management. But even when all thought of farming had gone, it was still vital for someone in the House to possess land agency expertise. The records are full of examples of Houses with incompetent Abbots accumulating heavy debts often from extravagant building projects but failing to manage their land effectively.

With luck, a competent man would follow a financial failure and by dint of good management restore the House finances. Prior Henry at Canterbury was an excellent example. In 1285, he took over a debt of £5,000. By shrewd attention to detail, as well as understanding the larger economic picture along with rigorous cost control, he bought finances to equilibrium by 1300 and then a surplus.

Fortunately for **Glastonbury**, though late in time, there was a monk of outstanding ability in land agency matters, Brother Thomas Sutton. He compiled Abbot Beer's terrier in 1515-16. Outside Cellarer was his official title but Estates Bursar would be the correct title today. He personally supervised the perambulations of all the 57 Glastonbury manors listing tenants, rents and acreages as well as other relevant details. There were no plans. Each estate was described by its bounds and it seems that local boys may have been taken on these expeditions and beaten at important markers to remind them of the boundaries and then 'had pennies stuffed in their mouths to stop their noise'. Leastwise, that happened in adjoining Dorset in later years. A full analysis of Abbot Beere's terrier may be found in the author's *Wealth & Estates of Glastonbury Abbey*. It is the most complete record extant of any monastic estate's rents and acres. It also covers the biggest – 130,000 acres – some 3 per cent of the monastic total.

Other monks, known as Obedientiaries, had useful but lesser management responsibilities. One such was the Medarius – the Honey Monk. His job was to ensure adequate supplies of honey from the various manors to satisfy his colleagues' sweet tooth and provide the raw material for mead and altar candles. (Candles made from beeswax were clean burning unlike rush lights using animal fat.) A major source of the honey for Glastonbury were the Brent Manors, land now better known as an M5 motorway service area. 'John Gyles pays 17s for his house, yard and 42 acres but in addition must pay to the Medarius 5 gallons of honey or 2s 6d' states the Beere terrier. In the same area, some three miles south of junction 22 on the east side of the motorway, just over the Huntspill river lies Withy Farm. This was Glastonbury's tractor factory or rather specialist ox breeding unit when the Glastonbury monks were serious about farming.

At the suppression of Butleigh, another Glastonbury manor, a memorandum was noted to:

> advertyce Mr Surveyor how the Kings tenauntes of his Grace's manor complayneth that Mr Strangwais tenaunt of Compton Donden oppresseth the commens with more cattell than they can keep upon their tenures in winter … and desire for the reformacon thereof that it will please the said Mr Surveyor to write unto the said Mr Stangwais that he may cause a redress.'

14 *West front of Peterborough Cathedral, 'the finest in christendom'. Some 60,000 acres supported the abbey activities including the extensive farming operations in early years outlined on pp.19 and 21.*

Plenty of other such complaints were found covering such matters as blocked rights of way and weirs 'put down'. Practical land and water management matters which had to be dealt with then as now and on the Somerset Levels perhaps better then than now (2014).

Human nature does not change. One poor monk recording such matters at Glastonbury tailed off his work with the sad marginal comment that 'my hands are so cold that I can write … no … more'.

By the end, virtually all monastic land was let on tenancies of varying lengths. The picture was one of quite tightly organised communities, out of touch with their *raison d'être* but working within time-honoured but often onerous rules with human attitudes little different from today. It was a money economy. The monks no longer farmed their land. They took cash rents in lieu of work with just small amounts of rents-in-kind when it suited them. Lay officials and advisers played an increasing part in the management of the estates and were thus very well placed at the Dissolution to apply to the Court of Augmentations for land they wished to buy.

MONASTIC WOODLAND

Timber was a vital part of the national and monastic economy. Wood was required for 'housebote, firebote, ploughbote, cartbote, hedgebote, foldbote' etc. Bote was the right and requirement for the tenants to take material for their own holdings and the maintenance of the abbey or priory estate. The extent of woodland on different properties varied greatly. Many Houses had substantial and often very valuable surplus mature timber to sell. Others were reported as '*Bosc' nul*'. Overall, monastic woods probably represented some 5-6 per cent of land in addition to the agricultural area, down from 15 per cent at the Domesday Survey.

As a general rule, the monks kept all timber in their own hands and this was usually a valuable asset – 'grete okys' being worth 'vjs viiid' (6s. 8d.) each on Glastonbury's Buckland Newton estate in Dorset. On other properties there might be hardly enough timber for the essential needs of the estate and so no saleable surplus. Hence 'Bosc'nul'. It was not until the Court of Augmentations, with their specialist forestry department, got to grips with the sale of woodland that precise measurements of areas were made but it would be impossible accurately to co-ordinate all the multitudinous woodland sales made subsequent to the Dissolution. A very detailed valuation of the woods of the wealthy **Abingdon Abbey**, Berkshire has survived. It covered some 1,197 acres and 24,000 trees, with a further 400 acres and 21,000 trees noted but excluded. This was less than three per cent of the estimated total estate of some 60,000 acres. The woods were run on the clear policy of 'coppice and standards'. The coppice underwood, usually hazel or sweet chestnut, was cut at regular intervals while the standard trees were left to grow to maturity, 100 years or more. Mature trees ready to fell were valued at up to 2s. 8d. apiece, rather less than the great oaks of Glastonbury.

Income per acre was often averaged by the Court of Augmentations and 6d.-1s./ acre was a common range. This would be the income per acre averaged over the estimated life of the wood. Clearly, the income from a clear felled acre of 100-year oak would have to be averaged over 100 years to give an annual estimate.

Capital values were easier to estimate as there would be buyers for timber offered for sale. The Suppression accounts sometimes gave very full capital values. The Leicestershire commissioners went into particular detail. One such was well wooded **Ulverscroft**, an Augustinian priory. There on the demesne, scattered trees were put at £23 plus 10 acres of 'thick' (ie unthinned) wood 10 years old; 42 acres at 30 years plus; 170 acres at 50 years plus; 30 acres at 80 years plus and 207 acres at 100 years plus. Total value £745 to give an average capital value for growing timber, managed on a long rotation, of £1 11s. per acre – on 459 acres out of an estate total of some 2,000 acres. At **Garendon**, a Cistercian House, 549 acres averaged £1 3s. per acre on 13 per cent of the estimated 5,300 acres. Compared with these, the Augustinian nunnery of **Grace Dieu** was a mess. 196 acres of similar aged trees were valued at only £79 – 8s. per acre. The woods were seven per cent of the total, close to the estimated national average. The Abingdon figures showed an average capital value of £2 9s. per acre but areas that had recently been clear felled of both of coppice and high timber were valued at nothing.

Tenants' rights to take firewood were regulated by custom. The phrase, still use today, 'By hook and by crook' referred to wood that could be reached and cut in this way.

There was, however, another element of woodland economy, generally in the hands of the tenants. This today might be known as short rotation coppice destined for biofuels. Many tenancy agreements provided for an area of alder, hazel or sweet chestnut. This would be for hedging and fencing as well as burning. These woods would be coppiced every ten or fifteen years with rapid re-growth from the stools. Mature trees might also be regularly pollarded to provide wood and leafy forage for cattle. Wattle hurdles, an essential part of sheep husbandry, would be made from split hazel coppice. The surveyors producing the Suppression accounts for Glastonbury neatly defined coppicing as an activity which did not 'mynyshe spoyle nor hurt but the woods to contyinue as they are nowe'.

The last residue of the traditional coppice industry remains in Kent where split (cleft) chestnut paling fencing is still in demand.

Vineyards

In the early years of the millennium, the monasteries were the mainstay of a flourishing wine-producing activity, not just for Holy Communion but also for regular drinking if records of monastic living can be trusted. Monastic vineyards were concentrated in Worcestershire, Gloucestershire, Kent, Surrey, Sussex and Hampshire. Over 20 have been identified in Worcestershire, producing a 'sort of English Bordeaux'. Westminster had a vineyard at Deerhurst, Gloucester. Other major Benedictine Houses known to have vineyards were St Albans, Canterbury, Glastonbury, Abingdon, Bury St Edmunds, Norwich, Peterborough, Thorney, Rochester, St Mary's York, Ely and Winchester. The largest vineyard identified was not in any of these counties but in Bedfordshire at Old Warden where the Suppression accounts

15 & 16 *Monks at work. Twelfth-century Cistercian wood choppers and a cellarer with important responsibilities.*

listed a '1 close called le greate Vyneyard, lytell Vyneyard & le barton (yard) cont. 50 acs.' There were economic incentives for the establishment of English vineyards. Imported wine was expensive and the post-Conquest influx of French wine drinking abbots and monks pushed up demand. If this could be met from home production, so much the better for the cellar's accounts. However, by the Dissolution, the vineyards had almost all gone. The lack of staff willing to tend the vines and cheaper imports were the main reason, not the climate.

Desmond Seward's book *Monks and Wine* is a very full account of English and continental monastic viticulture.

6

Monastic Finance and Debts

'I trusted so much that I sold the skinne before the beast was taken, setting down in
my books what afterwards was a desperate debt'.
Euphues. John Laly.

'Proportion thy expenses to what thou hast in possession not to thy expectancies;
otherwise he that feeds on wind must needs be griped with the cholic at last.'
Adages and Proverbs. Rev. Thomas Fuller.

These two little homilies encapsulate just about all that went right and went wrong
with monastic finance. There are plenty of examples of financial incompetence and
several of unusual financial competence among individual Houses but what was the
position for the monastic estate as a whole? Earlier self-inflicted problems arising
from unwise forward selling of wool, sometimes years before the fleece was sheared,
and extravagant building programmes have been noted. The income side was a matter
of collecting rents due and farm profits when earned. Therein lay the problem; when
pestilence struck the livestock and harvests failed – matters over which the monks had
no control. Prayers did not solve the problem when famine loomed. The steady move
from farming to letting removed the risk of day-to-day farming but diseases of crops
and stock certainly affected tenants' ability to pay their rents.

Levels of debt at many monasteries were heavy in the 13th century and took many
years to repay. At **Meaux**, a Cistercian abbey in east Yorkshire, Abbot Robert resigned in
1280 leaving a debt of £3,678 (perhaps two years' gross rental), money borrowed from
Italian wool merchants and English bankers. It took his successor Abbot Richard over 30
years to reduce the debt to £1,169. **Fountains** was bankrupt around 1280 mainly through
the heavy forward selling of wool to fund current extravagances. Uniquely, the property
was mortgaged to the Italian wool merchants but bailed out by the State as too important
to fail. These abbots lived too soon to appreciate the cautions heading this chapter. There
were many monastic Houses at the time who obviously lacked the expertise to run their
business affairs. When brought to book, the main result was often a shrinkage in monk
numbers and a run down of the property as sale of freeholds was not an option. **Rievaulx**,
impecunious in later years, had buildings in a poor state when the Earl of Rutland took
them on in 1540, the spire and crossing tower having collapsed.

In the main, the monasteries worked through their early financial woes by improved
management in the 15th and 16th centuries. So they should, with such a massive
endowment of property free of mortgage and rent.

At the Dissolution, the position was generally one of only modest and manageable
debt, not because the monks were unwilling to borrow but because lenders closed
their purses as people could see how matters were developing.

Prof. Savine puts this very well:

> Institutions and corporations that are uncertain of their existence from day to day do not readily obtain large credit … the proximity of Suppression was not a secret to the neighbouring population and local capitalists became sceptical with regard to the chances of recovering money lent to the monks. The monks might assure their neighbours as much as they liked that the interests of other people would not suffer by the Suppression; the neighbours nevertheless had serious grounds for fearing that contracts with the monks entered into on the eve of Dissolution would be declared void as having been contracted in bad faith.

What actually happened was that movable assets, particularly livestock and valuables, often 'walked', with the proceeds being used either to pay pressing creditors or hidden away against the day of nemesis. But compared with both the value of the freeholds and the extent of annual incomes, few Houses had heavy debts and many had monies owing and collectable. A debt of as much as half a year's income was relatively uncommon and could therefore be paid by the Court of Augmentations with half a year's income less unavoidable liabilities such as agreed pensions. The Court did look at transactions or evidence of bad faith but generally paid out on all claims that looked genuine. Lack of spare cash to continue operations was a major incentive to surrender a House and gain a pension. **Stoneleigh** (Warwicks) was an example of a heavy debt. It owed £219 9s. to 36 creditors, some of long standing. The net annual income was just £151. It would therefore take close to 18 months to pay off that debt.

7

Monastic Charity versus Chastity

*Were the 'religious' pious, charitable men and women giving their lives to prayer,
study, doles for the poor and other good works or were they idle folk given to
promiscuous sex while living off the fat of the land? Or were there many examples
of human behaviour at and between these extremes? Where did the balance lie?*

Monastic charity, though usually given by apologists of the system as its main
justification, is difficult to track down. On some analyses, it was less than three per
cent of income. There were compulsory alms specified by original donors but these
were often distributions of food on specific days – not much use to a pauper needing
sustenance on a regular basis. Random help to weary travellers, also frequently
mentioned, does not seem sufficient justification for the maintenance of a large
monastery.

It is probable that the system of corrodians was an important element of monastic
charity. Under the system, poor people could be taken in, housed and fed indefinitely.
The same service was available to the well off but they were expected to pay directly
or indirectly. The Crown and Founders' relatives often made use of this provision.
In 1532, for a one-off payment of £20, an elderly couple were taken in by the
Augustinian nuns of **Grace Dieu** who promised to feed them on a specified diet for
the rest of their lives along with the same provision for their four cows and two pigs
who were also taken in. (£20 might have represented the rent from 150 acres over five
years, perhaps £50,000 in today's money.) The Nunnery was suppressed in October
1538 so what happened to this couple? The House also ran a 'hospital' for 12 poor
people. What happened to them?

In this way, some monasteries had provided a real, if limited, care home service
which ended at the Dissolution. Some sympathy has in the past been expressed for
monks who lost their occupation but they often got a pension. Little has been heard
about the fate of the corrodians thrown out by the closure and demolition of their
home.

Hospitals were founded by the monks and the Augustinians had something of
a reputation for this work. In London, **St Bartholomew's** and **St Thomas's** were
Augustinian foundations. The latter catered for the poor, sick and homeless and Sir
Richard (Dick) Whittington endowed a maternity ward for unmarried mothers.

Prof. Savine calculated that possibly as many as 35,000 non 'religious' people were
fed by the monasteries at the suppression but these included outside workers, inside
servants and officials and certainly not all corrodians. To make a guess, if there were,

say, an average of four corrodians per monastery, the total might have been some 2,000 people.

All in all, temporary aid to travellers, regular and required charitable donations, other random charitable donations, modest regular alms (crumbs from a rich monk's table) and the semi-permanent provision of care home accommodation do not seem enough to warrant a claim that the monks and nuns played an important part nationally in relieving distress.

So, if they were not being very charitable, what did the monks and nuns get up to? If asked the question at the beginning of the 16th century, the honest ones would probably have said, 'We are just hanging on in here'. Were they just another organisation professing charitable motives but being run for themselves by themselves without reference to their original purpose? Any examples of this amongst our present-day charities?

We know about the clerical and artistic work in the cloister, the perpetual and often irksome daily round of prayers and outdoor labour. We also know about the grand lifestyle of the Heads of the larger Houses and we also know about human nature, more perhaps than St Benedict would admit to. Tales of scandalous monastic behaviour were rife and it seems often justified. At **Glastonbury**, years after the Dissolution, there was a verbatim report of a secret passage from the abbey to the vaults of the adjoining George and Pilgrim Hotel,

> with staires by which wee ascend to the Abbots chamber very privately. In the chamber is a fayre Ancient Bedsteed wrought and gilded finely, here the Abbot, by the vault, often came to this Inne and this chamber to Exercise himself Ad purgandos Renes (for the purging of his loins). The man of the house, Mr Dorvell told mee that this bedsteed … is always reserved, on his lease, for the King to use at his pleasure and in this room they say K.H.8 once lay.

The author has seen the walled-up end of the passage but can confirm no other details.

However, what is not in doubt is the substance of just one of the Glastonbury properties held in hand for the pleasure of the abbot of the time. At Pilton, now the annual site of a different sort of merrymaking, there was,

> a feyr curtilage, walled with a feyr gatehouse, a feyr open hall with hearth, 2 porches, 10 feyr chambers, a long chapel with bellhops, a wyne cellar, a pretty pantry & butry, a feyr kitchen & larder, a bake house, a woodhouse, a stabull for 10 horses, a feyr pichyn house and orchard and garden adjoining the parke of wood and good pasture containing in circuit 3 miles (350-400 acres) plenysshed with 350 deer and a feyr stream running through the same.

Such was the site of today's **Glastonbury Festival** as surveyed by the King's Commissioners in 1539.

At **Cerne**, Dorset, there was worse. In 1535, a dissident monk, William Christchurch, listed complaints against Abbot Thomas Corton and sent them direct to Thomas Cromwell. No need for Cromwell to look further for misdeeds sufficient to suppress the monastery:

> For keeping concubines in the cellar of the abbey and especially Joan Postell
> For letting the church and lands go to ruin
> For wasting the goods of the monastery on his concubines and children and giving them great gifts

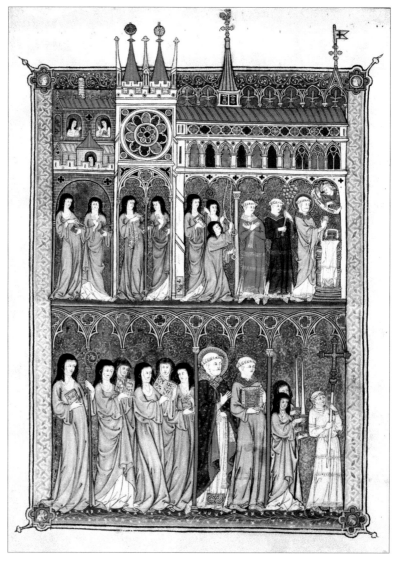

17   *The good nuns. The abbess of La Sainte Abbaye with her staff and book (fifth from left) about to celebrate mass c.1300. On the ground floor, a procession of priest, acolytes and nuns carrying music books and candles.*

18   *Naughty monk and nun in the stocks for a misdemeanour we can only guess at guess at in view of her companion.*

For giving sumptuous gifts to a son he had by a former concubine Joan Gardeners

For maintaining another son called Harry whom he begat on Alice Roberts 'to the great slander of our religion'

He had a man child by one Edith, servant to Nicholas Foway

He openly solicits honest women in the town and elsewhere to have his will of them

His concubines sit at table with him

His brother and others of his kindred bear rule in the monastery to the disquiet of the monks

The abbot does not keep obits and the doles

He allows two of his monks who daily haunt queens, to celebrate mass without confession

He allows some monks to play cards all night and celebrate mass in the morning

He has abolished some masses

He allows women to stay with the brethren from noon to evensong

He has several times imprisoned William Christchurch for writing and speaking against him

He expelled William Christchurch from the monastery and sent him to the prior of Monmouth where he was very ill handled.

Cerne Abbey Historical Society

A monastic whistle-blower with a vengeance. Like other whistle-blowers today, he was not rewarded for his efforts at rooting out corruption – he was not on the list of pensioners at the suppression. There must be some truth in his allegations because he would know that he could be cross-examined on his testimony. His list probably encompasses most of the sins of which the monks and abbots have often been accused. Apart, that is, from active banditry, a charge levelled at the monks of **Dieulacres** in Staffordshire. At **Ramsey**, Huntingdon, monkish morals were none too straightforward – a visiting bishop in the 15th century remonstrated with certain of the brethren for taking fields in their own name and 'out of liking' hiring women of uncertain virtue to do the work. Monastic discipline for sinning monks included imprisonment, banishment to a distant house with a harsh regime, and beating – an effective metal scourge has been unearthed at **Rievaulx**.

But enough of this scandal and unpleasantness. What are the conclusions about the lives of the 'religious'?

Some good, some bad but on balance not enough good to justify holding on to 16 per cent of England's productive land. For once, the author agrees with Henry VIII.

8

How it all Ended

Henry VIII came to the throne in April 1509 at the age of seventeen. By that time, it was clear that there was dead wood in the monasteries if not downright rotten timber. **Cardinal Wolsey**, the son of an Ipswich butcher and graduate of Magdalen College, Oxford (there is 16th-century social mobility) was a key adviser to Henry VII and just about ran the country in the early years of Henry VIII. He was well aware of both the problems but mainly of the opportunities that lay in the monastic realm. As Archbishop of York and Lord Chancellor, he was in a position to act decisively. He did so especially in the matter of creating great personal wealth which ultimately aided his downfall. The gift to the King of Hampton Court Palace, which he had built for himself, did not prevent his fall from grace but he died before the Axe man could get him.

With Cromwell already on hand to learn the business, Wolsey dissolved some 30 smaller religious houses between 1524 and his death in 1530. The alleged purpose was reform, the funds raised were used to fund Cardinal's College, Oxford and a school at Ipswich. But these, seen mainly as personal monuments, did not survive him. Cardinal College was re-founded by Henry VIII as Christ Church and Ipswich demolished. This early monastic Dissolution was a significant object lesson to **Thomas Cromwell**. He learnt it well.

There is debate as to whether the King led Cromwell or Cromwell the King in the matter of the final dissolution. It seems probable that Cromwell had the ideas and the King confirmed them. Cromwell's start in life was not propitious. He was the son of a Putney smith and admitted to being a bit of a ruffian in his younger days. He went abroad, spending some years on the continent where he honed latent skills as a linguist, trader, lawyer and financier. He returned to England in 1512 and joined Wolsey's staff in 1520. Politically he became the most powerful man in the land after the King and never looked back until that fateful day in June 1540 when, as he took his seat at a Privy Council meeting, he was accused of treachery by the Duke of Norfolk and forcibly removed to the Tower by the Captain of the Guard. All obviously a put up job but done with the King's prior agreement. Cromwell had done a brilliant job in dissolving the monasteries, adding greatly to the national and royal treasury as well as reforming the machinery of state. But gratitude in Tudor times, as well as now, can be a lively sense of favours to come. Cromwell, having failed in the marriage-broking department (Anne of Cleves was a disaster as a potential bride), was deemed to be of no further help to the King and was hated by many conservative counsellors. Snobbery played a part – the indictment included *Scandalum magnatum* – bring the nobility into disrepute. This was disingenuous – ennobled landed men could be created at the stroke of a quill and confirmed by royal seal and equally easily removed by a blow of the executioner's axe. No trial for Cromwell, condemned by Act of Parliament, and executed on 23 July, some say with intentional barbarous inefficiency. Axe men could be so persuaded and if the King was agin' him, Cromwell had no friends. However, it seems that the King soon came to regret the loss of a key adviser.

The Dissolution proper started with the 1536 Act of Suppression but the ground had been well prepared by Cromwell's Visitors. Their job was to find dirt, whether there or not. This Act nationalised only Houses with a net temporal income of less than £200 a year. The actual wording of the preamble was:

> An Act whereby all Religious Houses of Monks, Canons and Nuns which may not dispend Manors, Lands, Tenements and Hereditaments above the clear yearly value of £200 are given to the King's Highness, his heirs and successors for ever.

Spiritual income was excluded – net temporal income would seem to have been the measure.

There follows the notorious and hypocritical rant:

> Forasmuch as manifest sin, vicious, carnal and abominable living is daily used and committed among little and small abbeys … where the congregation of such religious persons is under the number of twelve persons whereby the governors of such religious houses … spoil, destroy, consume and utterly waste as well their churches … houses, farms, granges, lands … and unless such small houses be utterly suppressed and the religious persons therein committed to great and honourable monasteries in this realm … there can be no reformation …

With abbots in attendance and saying nothing, this extraordinary piece of legislation was passed by Parliament and the work began. The requirements of the Act concerning payments of debts, pensions and like matters do, however, seem to have been adhered to. The Act applied to only about 30 per cent of the Houses but out in the country, especially in the north, it added to existing considerable discontent. This in turn led to **The Pilgrimage of Grace** or **The Lincolnshire Rising** depending on your viewpoint. This, backed by gentry, monks and artisans, was the only serious opposition to the Dissolution. After meeting with the rebels, the King's men, including Norfolk, promised pardons and after only a few weeks the rebellion was over. Of course the Crown broke its word on the pretext that the pardons were offered under duress. Eight aristocrats and five abbots were summarily executed including the abbots of Fountains and Jervaulx. 76 others were executed in Carlisle and the final death toll included a further 104 executions as trials, with only a few acquittals, got under way. Some 30,000 were reputed to have taken part in the revolts. Perhaps a survival rate of over 99 per cent of those who had actively opposed the King's policies was not bad. However, it was clear that in no way would the King compromise on the Dissolution policy.

It was not long before the total hypocrisy of the 1536 Act was exposed. Members of 'great' abbeys, previously confirmed as places 'where religion was right well kept', were soon having to admit in writing that their way of life was 'no more than a vain and superstitious round of dumb ceremonies' which they now wished to abandon and live as true Christian men. Whitehall had dictated the end of monasticism. Full stop.

Glastonbury provides a miserable example of how badly Cromwell's unscrupulous agents could behave. As the richest house, the King wanted the abbey assets, if by attainder (alleged treason), then so much the better as the assets would by-pass the Court of Augmentations and go straight to the royal coffers. The most unsavoury Thomas Moyle and Richard Pollard along with notorious Dr Richard Layton reported to Cromwell on 23 September 1539: 'We examined him (the abbot) on certain articles and as his answers were not to our purpose we advised him to call to his remembrance that which he had then forgotten' … but the sick and aged Abbot Whyting would confess to 'no more gold' and was given a traitor's death with his head impaled on the abbey gate. Henry VIII's England was often an uncivilised place.

Two Treasury monks, Roger Jacob and John Thorne, were hanged as being thought to be complicit in hiding abbey assets – a matter of which Whyting would not have been aware. There is evidence for the hiding of abbey treasure from over 100 years later:

> Where the porters lodge of the abbey once was is now a good habitable house the master of which about 30 years since pulled down a mantle piece of a chimney and laid it out in the street where it lay severrall years, he was in price once to sell it asking but ten groats for it but the chapman would give but three shillings. At length his daughter being to build a little chamber, shee got a workman to cut it out to make staires, he trying the stone to see if it was sound found a hole wherein was above four score pieces of gold of severrell bignesses, the woman got 70 pieces and she told me the mason kept many more …'
>
> (Bristol Records Office 36074 located by Edwin George.)

All monasteries now doubted their future and a succession of voluntary surrenders took place, led by Furness where support for the rising had been suspected but not proved. Abbot Robert Pele, a weak and ineffectual man, was 'advised' by the King's emissary, Sir Robert Radcliffe, to surrender. Pele took the advice and a pension. A precedent was set and abbeys rapidly fell with only a few holding out to their serious detriment – the hangman for the abbot and doubtful pension provisions for the rest. A second Act for the Dissolution of Abbeys was passed in May 1539 but this was only to legitimise the voluntary surrenders and so ensure that the Crown's title to the confiscated land was good.

A self justification for surrender was put forward by a number of Houses and in law it could hold good. Under the 1534 Act of Supremacy the King had become Head of the Church in England and therefore in taking monastic land he was only taking what was his. The Pope was out of the loop. Robert Crowley, poet and printer (see chapter end) regretfully made this point. Furthermore, many houses were very short of cash and could not see their way forward financially. Surrender with a pension was therefore a relief to many.

Commissioners Lawson, Belasses and Blithman reporting from York on 15 December 1537 to 'Crumwell, ower most noble, singular good lord' on the surrenders of Northern Houses and asking for instruction as to the bells, stated that they had

> quyetly taken the surrenders of and dissolved the monasteries of Wyrkesop (Notts) Monkbretton, Sante Andrews in York, Byland, Ryvalle, Kirkham and Ellerton, the Fryers at Tykelland, Doncastere … we p'ceyved no murmure or grief in any behalf but were thankfully received

19   *Furness, Cumbria ended up as a Cistercian abbey second in wealth only to Fountains in that Order. The abbey held some 25-30,000 acres, some as far afield as the Isle of Man. It was the first abbey to surrender voluntarily, that or a hanging, a lead followed by most other abbeys. Wonderful red sandstone ruins remain.*

… as no doubt were the pensions that came with a constructive surrender. It seems that the monks had had enough of an unequal struggle. Famous Ryvalle/Rievaulx was caught in the first round of accusations of 'vicious and carnal living', not for its lack of morals but because it did not have a relevant income of more than £200. Today's spectacular ruins are no measure of the terminal penury of the abbey. Bolton Priory, with a relevant income of less than £200, should have been on this list but for some reason suppression was delayed.

The last traditional House to go was Augustinian Waltham Holy Cross in Essex. Robert Fuller surrendered in March 1540 with a pension. Some Hospitaller land lasted a little longer as did sundry small charities.

This finalised an amazing transfer of land, second only to the Norman Conquest. Some 10 per cent of the productive land of all England had changed hands in an orderly way, involving over 2,000 transactions, in barely five years – with a further 6 per cent over the next 50 years. The organisational skills of Thomas Cromwell were the chief reason for such a smooth transfer along with the active co-operation of the landed gentry who knew, understood and coveted the assets.

The original excuse in Cardinal Wolsey's day for the Dissolution was to re-distribute under-used monastic assets and use them for religious and educational developments. To an extent, this did happen. Cathedrals re-financed were Norwich, Winchester, Carlisle, Canterbury, Rochester and Ely. New cathedral foundations were Chester, Gloucester, Peterborough, Westminster (as a royal Peculiar), Oxford (Christchurch) and Bristol. Thus all these buildings escaped the demolition contractors (a good business in the 1540s) and survived for the greater glory of God and his new self-proclaimed Head of the Church in England under Christ.

Further grants went to the two archbishops and other episcopal interests. The largest collegiate beneficiaries were at Cambridge: Kings, Clare and St Michael's (Trinity). There was little cash so most of these bequests will have been as land, perhaps a total of some 700,000 acres. This will have been a re-distribution of existing land both in the case of cathedral re-foundations and the conversion of priories to cathedral status. At the beginning (1536-39), the King was generous to his chums. Twenty-one per cent of grants were gifts and most of these went in the first four years. The most noticeable recipients (and little good it did some of them) were Charles Brandon, Duke of Suffolk, 50,000 acres mainly in Lincolnshire, after exchanges but no close heirs surviving; Thomas Cromwell, very briefly Earl of Essex but lost the lot, possibly 50,000 acres, when he was executed and the King got it all back again; Thomas and Edward Seymour (Edward, later Lord Protector, had brother Thomas executed – treason was a good enough excuse and he had secretly married the King's widow Katherine Parr). Edward in turn was executed after a coup by disgruntled members of the Regency Council. Thomas Wriothesley did better as one time Lord Chancellor and later Earl of Southampton but a dodgy character thrown off the Privy Council. Winners included Lord John Russell with a gift of perhaps 25,000 acres and later Earl of Bedford, a Dukedom and **Woburn Abbey**; Thomas Manners, Earl of Rutland gained the 12,000-acre **Rievaulx** estate. He was a soldier chum of the King from actively working to suppress 'The Rising'. He also obtained ex-monastic land from Belvoir Priory and elsewhere and the family went on to a dukedom, seated at **Belvoir** Castle and some 70,000 acres at the end of the 19th century; Thomas Howard, Duke of Norfolk, and **Sir Richard Gresham**, the King's favourite financier, were also long-term gainers. Sir Richard completed the largest single transaction with the Court, buying the greater part of **Fountains Abbey** land along with **Swyne** and **Nunkeeling** nunneries also in Yorkshire, for £11,137 11s. 8d. in October 1540. The Gresham family made several further purchases in the 1540s and are remembered through Gresham Street in the City.

Later it was the Officials, particularly those in the Court of Augmentations, who were best placed to negotiate bargains. Perhaps 40,000 acres went in this way but it did not take long for some of the favoured courtiers to trade on or exchange their land, needing money or wanting a more compact estate. The London men were mainly either agents acting for others in the country or speculators spotting a bargain when the King needed cash. Lawyers came into both categories. Perhaps 35,000 acres went in this way, much of it rapidly moved on to final buyers. The gentry and yeomen probably gained 40,000 acres in this first round and most of it will have stuck, some to the present day.

There were well over 1,000 individuals taking advantage of this first round of the Dissolution sales and many more after trading. The reigns of Edward VI, Bloody

20 *The Cellarium – Fountains Abbey. Used for food, drink and general storage, it was over 300ft long and no comparable monastic building remains. The scale of this store is best appreciated from the illustration on page 72.*

Mary and Elizabeth saw the remaining 1.3 million acres go. In fact there was a little more land as many chantries and cells, yet to be sold up, had small land endowments.

The Russells were one of the most successful families in retaining their monastic acquisitions and increasing them. Russell, Tavistock and Bedford Squares in London bear witness to their successful urban diversification. However, many country families have also held on, in a more modest way, to ex-monastic land acquired before the great inflations. If land was worth 10s/ acre in 1540, it is now (2014) worth £5-7,000 /acre. But, sobering thought, a lot of land in England was worth little more than £10-£20/acre in the 1930s.

EPILOGUE

Land and the profits therefrom was what mattered to King, courtiers and more humble subjects. By establishing an estimate of land holdings as opposed to the more usual financial estimates of monastic interests, it is hoped that a wider appreciation of the effects of the Dissolution may be obtained. Acres are constant. Money values are not. The estimate of the monastic estate which is put forward is 4 million acres – 16 per cent of rural England and 13 per cent of the whole country. The margin for error in this estimate is considerable. However, it is thought that it could err on the low side.

An average Dissolution rent of 6.5d/acre is suggested for the rural estate with demesne rents around 13d/acre and customary rents 4-5d/acre. Capital values are put at around 10s/acre (50p) for the disposals made up to the end of the reign of Henry VIII. These figures imply an investment return to the buyers of monastic land of 5-6 per cent. The average monastic estate was some 8,000 acres, a tidy property then and now.

The population of England at the Dissolution was around 2.5 million. The religious community was some 10,000 decreasing to say 7,000 as the Dissolution loomed. These figures excluded the servants and lay officers most of whom would have a job whoever owned the land. The religious, who represented less than four in 1,000, had the final disposition of the net benefit from around 16 per cent of productive English land. This, allied to the King's need for money and the discrediting of the monastic ideal by the monks' own actions and such opinion-formers as Erasmus and Luther, virtually ensured that the monasteries would not survive.

The desecration of the architectural glories which had resulted from the monastic heritage was a sad consequence. We do, however, have a few cathedrals left to show what existed before the demolition contractors moved in. Imagine wrecking balls, dynamite and diggers moving in today on say Durham, Worcester or Peterborough cathedrals as Henry VIII and Thomas Cromwell so nearly ordered. Clouds of dust, random heaps of stone and roaring fires to burn the roofing timbers and melt the lead.

With 10 per cent of productive England changing ownership by the end of the reign of Henry VIII and the remaining 5 per cent by the end of the reign of Elizabeth I, the grand design for the finances of the state in the mind of Thomas Cromwell failed. Did Henry VIII not understand or not care? If the bulk of the monastic estate had been preserved as a permanent investment for the Crown, the whole problem of taxation which arose in Stuart times and the civil war which resulted might never have occurred.

However, what actually happened was probably a greater gain in terms of political stability. In addition to increasing the spread of existing owners, probably by well over 2,000, land was made available to a new, wider class of people who thus had a greater interest in political stability and the property rights which go with this. This may well have helped stave off more violent revolution such as that later suffered by France.

The Dissolution weakened the hold of the Roman Catholic Church. Those who had received land were fearful that it might be confiscated under an RC regime. The Gentlemen of England would have none of this. Their property rights would take precedence over mere religion. However, many of the recipients of gifts and sales of land – those close to King Henry – may have prudently morphed into country gentlemen during the uncertainties of the brief reign of Edward VI and Catholic 'Bloody Mary' which followed his death. Elizabeth I re-established a protestant ascendancy which heralded times of more stable property rights.

Temporary aid to travellers, regular and required charitable donations, other random charitable donations, modest regular alms and the semi-permanent provision of care-home accommodation do not seem enough to warrant a claim that the monks and nuns played an important part nationally in relieving distress. As to the monks and nuns themselves, there were some good, some bad, but on balance not enough good to justify holding on to nearly one sixth of productive English land.

Those actually working the land will have been little affected by a change in their masters. Their rents will have tended to go up but they may well have obtained improvements to their holdings not previously provided by the conservative 'religious'. Local tradesmen will have missed the monastic spend when income was centralised at the Court of Augmentations but an ultimate private local purchaser of an estate may well have spent most of the rent money in the district.

It is quite possible that the lubricant of a distribution of four million acres lessened the social upheaval which might otherwise have been expected from the violent changes to Church and State put in hand by Henry VIII, a King who, by the end of his life, proved himself quite unfit to exercise power. He had become a nasty, vindictive, ungrateful tyrant.

Dispersal of the monastic estate was certainly a wasted opportunity with most of the money squandered by the King, but not a disaster for the English Nation or the English Church. It was, however, a big boost for the landowning classes.

Certain Houses in each county have been selected on a rather arbitrary basis for a look in greater depth. Space would not allow this treatment of all the Houses warranting it.

A Selection of Houses from each County

Bedfordshire: Woburn, Old Warden and Elstow
Berkshire: Reading and Abingdon
Buckinghamshire: Missenden and Notley
Cambridge: Ely and Thorney
Cheshire: St Werburgh, Chester and Vale Royal
Cornwall: Launceston and Bodmin
Cumbria: Furness, Holm Cultram, Lanercost and Shap.
Derby: Darley and Dale.
Devon: Buckland, Buckfastleigh, Tavistock and Plymton
Dorset: Shaftesbury , Sherbourne, Milton and Cerne
Durham: Cathedral, Finchale and Jarrow
Essex: Waltham, St Osyth, St Botolphs Colchester, Berden and Heddingham
Gloucester : St Peters, Tewkesbury and Cirencester
Hampshire: Winchester, Hyde, Romsey and Beaulieu
Hereford: Abbey Dore and Wigmore
Hertford: St Albans
Huntingdon: Ramsey
Kent: Canterbury, Rochester and Sheppey
Lancashire: Whalley and Sawley
Leicester: St Mary's and Croxton
Lincolnshire: Crowland, Revesby and Sempringham
London and **Middlesex**: Westminster and Syon
Norfolk: Castle Acre, Norwich, and Walsingham
Northamptonshire: Peterborough and Catesby
Northumberland: Alnwick, Hexham, Hulne, Lindisfarne, Farne Isles and Tynemouth
Nottingham: Rufford, Thurgarton, Newstead, Worksop and Welbeck
Oxford: Oseney, Eynsham, Goring, Dorchester and Christchurch (St Frideswide's)
Shropshire: Bromfield, Chirbury, Wombridge, Shrewsbury, Wenlock and Haughmond
Somerset: Glastonbury, Cleeve, and Muchleney
Stafford: Burton on Trent, Croxden, Tutbury and Dieulacres
Suffolk: Bury St Edmunds, Butley and Leiston
Surrey: Merton, Shene, Chertsey, Southwark, Bermondsey, Tandridge, Reigate and Waverley
Sussex: Battle, Lewes, Michelham, Bayham and Boxgrove
Warwick: Coventry, Stoneleigh and Kenilworth
Wiltshire: Wilton, Malmesbury, Lacock and Amesbury
Worcester: Cathedral, Evesham and Pershore
Yorkshire: St Mary's York, Fountains, Rievaulx, Mount Grace, Byland and mention of Selby, Guisburn, Jervaulx, Bridlington and Whitby.

NOTE

The acreage estimates which follow are generally based on the assumption of a 6.5d/acre average rent and the Valor figure for gross temporal income reduced by 10 per cent to allow for non-agricultural income. The figures admit to a wide margin of error for individual monasteries especially in relation to soil quality but are thought to be a fair approximation for the counties and country.

BEDFORD

Not a major monastic county but with two substantial monasteries and a well-endowed nunnery. At **Woburn**, the Abbot came to an unfortunate death at the end of a rope as he openly preferred the Pope to the King as his spiritual overlord. There were possibly around 10-12,000 acres or a little more which came to the Russell family, up from the West country and in favour for their activities in keeping order down there. The family now grace society as Dukes of Bedford and are best known as safari park proprietors. The Russells had their fortune founded on a gift from the King made on 4 July 1539 of some 25,000 acres from **Tavistock** Abbey lands in Devon. These were valued at £1,050 per annum with a capital value of perhaps £21,000 if valued at 20 years' purchase, as was standard practice. Lord John Russell also bought another 25,000 acres or thereabouts at market prices. Near the end of the 19th century, the family were the third largest landowners in England with some 85,000 acres of which perhaps half may have come from the monastic estate in the 16th century.

Old Warden, slightly bigger than Woburn, returned a 50-acre vineyard to the King's Commissioners and money-earning water and wind mills amongst other assets. Mill rentals came to some £38, the highest found for any House. Land rentals were in line with averages apart from meadow which was low. 420 acres of arable were priced at 6d/acre, 203 acres pasture at 11d/acre and 40 acres meadow 14d/acre. The estate now comprises some 4,600 acres and is the home of an agricultural college, a pleasure park and the Shuttleworth Collection of cars and aircraft. At **Elstow**, Bishop Longland of Lincoln had cause, in 1531, to chide the nuns for their inappropriate dress sense … 'ther gownes and kyrtells be close afore and not so depe voyed at the breste and no more to use red stomachers' … cleavage problems and opportunities in the 16th century.

BERKSHIRE

The two largest Houses were Benedictine **Reading** and **Abingdon**. In terms of net income, they ranked sixth (£1,939) and seventh (£1,877) but the abbeys came to very different ends. At Abingdon, the Abbot, Thomas Pentecost, saw matters the King's way, surrendered the abbey and received the manor of Cumnor as a pension. At Reading, founded by Henry I in memory of his father, William the Conqueror, the Abbot, Hugh Faringdon, did not see matters the King's way. He was hanged and dismembered on Thomas Cromwell's orders and the Abbey property forfeited to the King. State papers of 26 June 1540 report gold and jewels from Glaston and Reading delivered to John Williams, master of the King's jewels.

BUCKINGHAMSHIRE

The county was not well endowed with religious houses. The two largest were Missenden and Notley, both Augustinian. (The Augustinians tended to get out and about more than the other Orders.) **Missenden**, a few miles north of High Wycombe, had perhaps about 7,000 acres of which 344 were demesne. **Notley**, north of Thame, had something over 6,000 acres. In the Suppression accounts, the demesne of 110 acres included 1 feld, stony and barren at 4d/acre. The auditors put the whole at 6d/acre and it seems this figure became common for a range of suppressed houses – a short cut by busy clerks in the Court of Augmentations?

Cambridge

Deep in the fens, on its Isle, **Ely** cathedral priory was ranked 18th on net income with perhaps 35,000 acres. (But the Bishop of Ely seems to have accumulated twice as much land as the Abbot.) The first grants of land to the monastery were 60 hides followed by 20 hides by King Edgar in 970. (A hide was originally a unit for taxation, but otherwise the amount of land which could be ploughed, seasonally, in a year by an eight-ox team. It varied between 80 and 160 acres depending on soil type and terrain. An oxgang or bovate represented an eighth of an acre – 10-20 acres depending on the soil. On difficult ground, the oxgang could be as little as five acres.) Thus the original pre-Conquest grants may have been 9-10,000 acres around the Isle and included a grant from surrounding vills of 10,000 eels a year. Who did the counting? Ely, though never very wealthy, had a generally sound monastic life and at the Dissolution, by royal favour, the Abbot and monks were translated to Dean and Chapter and so the abbey survives intact to this day as an awe-inspiring but friendly cathedral known locally as the Ship of the Fens. Included in the Abbey's investment portfolio were Mepal, Trumpington, Fulbourn, Teversham, Pampisfield, Thriplow and Horningsea. King Edgar also included a grant of woods at Hatfield, as Ely was and is short on woods. Carting timber 50 miles into Ely would have been a real sweat – boon work forced on reluctant tenants and struggling oxen.

Though an abbey in its own right, **Thorney** was associated with Peterborough from early times. According to the Anglo-Saxon Chronicle, in 656 Abbot Seaxwulf, who had already been given a most generous bequest of land for Medehamstede (Peterborough), had the nerve to ask for more – an anchorite cell for rest and meditation. King Wulfhere granted the request with the wish that the heavenly gatekeeper might diminish anyone who diminished the benefaction. In this way the Thorney site came initially to the Abbey. Matters did not go according to plan and Bishop Ethelwold had to buy the site back in 972 from a woman, diminished or not, named Ethelfled who had somehow acquired it. The site had become thoroughly overgrown with thorns and nettles, hence the name. The estate owned by the abbey in Cambridgeshire was Whittlesey given by the same Ethelwold and bought for 90 pounds of silver. By the Dissolution, the abbey had a temporal valuation of about £400 which could have represented some 12-15,000 acres, most of which was in Huntingdon and in the Yaxley and Stanground area. The abbey was originally a place for quiet meditation by monks on leave from Peterborough, helped no doubt by the home produced wine. William of Malmesbury, 13th-century, states that the vines were grown there along the ground or on low stakes as in the Medoc. The abbey is once again a peaceful and beautiful place as the A47 by-pass round Thorney village has finally opened.

Cheshire

The county boasted only six Houses, the largest of which was the Benedictine **St Werburgh** in Chester. The gross temporal income was put at £751 but Prof. Savine found evidence of slapdash work by the Valor Ecclesiasticus clerk in 1536 as to the

21 *Ely was a Benedictine priory which metamorphosed into a secular cathedral –*
thank goodness or thank God. Annual rents from its manors included 10,000 eels. In
the C15th, the North West transept collapsed, dodgy foundations, leaving the present
un- balanced appearance.

correct gross income. The abbey probably held of the order of 20-25,000 acres. The urban income was £71 10s. – nearly 10 per cent of the total. The abbey spent quite a lot on entertaining outsiders, £31. One recipient was the Earl of Derby who was paid £2 annually as steward. He held this office for seven other monasteries and the connection between landowners, aristocratic or gentry, played a large part in monastic life prior to, as well as at, the Dissolution. Those with inside knowledge stood a good chance of a profitable purchase from the Court of Augmentations. **Vale Royal** was a smaller, Cistercian house, east of Chester, close to Northwich, with perhaps 8,000 acres. It was a Royal house founded by Edward I in 1274-7 and endowed by him with a relic, allegedly part of the Cross, scrounged from the Holy Land. This did bring some pilgrims but not enough to build a big abbey. Remains of some abbey buildings are thought to be part of the local golf club's 19th hole.

Cornwall

Like Cheshire, Cornwall had only six monasteries. The two most prominent were both Augustinian priories. **Launceston**, to the east of Bodmin moor, probably had around 8,000 acres, the average for the whole country. The lands were mostly in the county at Kilkhampton, St Gennys, Stoke Climsland, Looe island with further ground at Pyworthy and Bradford in Devon. At the Dissolution, the buildings were acquired by one Garen Carew and used as stables, a bake house and piggeries. In 2008, Launceston Town council undertook a conservation and celebration of the ruins along with the Friends of Launceston Priory. Across the bleak moor to the west, **Bodmin** Priory can trace its foundation back to St Petroc in the 6th century. The name Bodmin comes from ancient Cornish – the house of the monks. With around 7,000 acres the priory was not wealthy but ruins survive and are looked after locally.

Cumbria (Cumberland and Westmorland)

Two Cistercian abbeys, **Furness** and **Holm Cultram**, were the major players. Furness was founded in 1124 by Stephen, Count of Blois, Duke of Lancaster and later a less than successful King. The House stayed in Royal favour and built up substantial assets with possibly around 27,000 acres, some in Yorkshire and disputed with Fountains, and some in Ireland and the Isle of Man. Demesne income was £105 – Fountains £183. The present substantial ruins, of warm red sandstone, are a credit to their medieval builders. The Abbey was a major power in the North West, surprising in view of its isolation. It is best remembered now, apart from the ruins, for its early 'voluntary' capitulation. Very many, if not most, abbeys followed this course. It could lead to a peaceful departure with a pension – the alternative was usually an unpleasant death as an alleged traitor to the King. On the coastal plain west of Carlisle, **Holm Cultram** may have had 10-12,000 acres and the River Waver for drainage. Remnants of the abbey are in use as the parish church.

Lanercost was one of the smaller Houses to survive. With a total income of only £80, having been bedevilled by Scots raiders and a Royal visit in 1306, it survives today, north-east of Carlisle, off the A69, as a romantic setting for local worship. At the Dissolution, there was probably little more than 1,000 acres to support the monks. The old county of Westmorland had the modest House of **Shap**, now the high point of the English motorway and rail network. There was a gross income of £160, a demesne income of £16 8s. and charitable giving of £5 18s. It is surprising

22   *Shap in the old county of Westmorland was one of the most isolated monasteries in the country but not the least well off, with a net income of £155. It was a Premonstratensian abbey on the west bank of the River Lowther, facilitating water in and effluent out – a necessity for every monastery. Much of the stone work went to build the now roofless Lowther Castle nearby.*

23   *Lanercost near Brampton, Cumbria, was a small lonely House with half the income enjoyed by Shap. The monks probably had little more than 1000 acres of reasonable land to support themselves. It was an Augustinian priory which saw much strife in early years – inevitable in view of proximity to the Scottish border. Now a quiet and beautiful location with the parish church in situ, our picture shows the priory wrapped in mist as it often will have been.*

that this figure was not higher in view of the claimed need to succour weary travellers on the track that is now the M6 and still a tricky road in a bad winter.

Derbyshire

The county is somewhat short on memorable monasteries but makes up for it with a good supply of memorable mansions – Chatsworth, Haddon Hall, Hardwick Hall, Bolsover Castle. **Darley**, an Augustinian abbey, was the largest House with maybe 8-9,000 acres. **Dale** was a smaller Premonstratensian abbey with perhaps 5,000 acres. The Derbyshire commissioners in the suppression accounts went into detail not always found elsewhere. Darley had 38 oxen, 10 cows, 9 horses, 52 pigs and 60 sheep. Leastwise this is what was there for the commissioners to count. What had walked off before they got there, who knows? There were also stocks of wheat, rye, barley, oats, malt, peas and hay. The stocks at Dale were similar but smaller. Creditors and debtors were listed. Dale owed £24 11s. 6d. with debtors put at £1. Darley owed £142 without any debtors.

Devon

Buckland was a modest Cistercian house. The site and demesne land went to Sir Richard Grenville in a deal which involved a gift from the King of £20. The area of the site and demesne sold to Grenville was 568 acres with an annual rent of £23 3s. 5d. However, the abbey held far more land than just the demesne sold to Grenville. This might have been 6-7,000 acres. Grenville's heirs sold to Sir Francis Drake, another well-known seafarer. **Plymton** and **Buckfastleigh** were the largest Houses in the county. **Tavistock** went to Lord John Russell as a gift of perhaps 25,000 acres for helping to keep the West Country in order. The land went to swell the future Bedford Estates enjoyed by Dukes yet to come, right up to the present day.

Dorset

The Benedictine abbey of **Shaftesbury** was far and away the richest House in the county with a net income of £1,150. It was also the second richest nunnery in the country after the Bridgettine **Syon** Abbey in Middlesex. Founded by Alfred the Great and his daughter Aethelgifu in 888, it grew to be a powerful institution but the nuns struggled with continuing financial worries. Domesday Book listed some 332 hides. Most of the manors were still owned at the Dissolution when the area was not less than 288 hides. At 120 acres/hide, this suggests that the abbey held upwards of around 35,000 acres. The last Abbess, Elizabeth Zouche and her 56 colleagues, held out as long as they dared but surrendered in March 1539, pocketing pensions. The abbey owned the largest 'tithe' barn in the country at **Tisbury** in Wiltshire (see page 2). (Technically a tithe barn existed only to hold the clerical tenth in a parish or manor.) The abbey site and perhaps 5,000 acres were sold to Sir Thomas Arundell for £2,167 giving him a rent of £131 and a yield of 6 per cent on his money. Second in the county on net income was Benedictine **Sherborne** with say 20,000 acres. **Cerne** was another Benedictine abbey probably with some 17,000 acres and founded in 987. The very phallic local Giant was probably not there to disturb the monks' thoughts as it is now thought to date only from the 17th century. Allegations of scandalous goings-on were reported to Cromwell by a dissident monk. The abbey was surrendered on 15 March 1539 to John Tregonwell, a King's commissioner. As an insider, Tregonwell later acquired buildings and land (2-3,000 acres?) of **Milton** (Middleton) Abbey, another Benedictine, Dorset House. He paid £1,000 on 23 February 1540 for an annual rental of £62 (6.2 per cent). He later made another purchase for £551 with a rental of £27 (4.9 per cent). The sites and remnants of both Sherborne and Milton are now schools.

Durham

Dominated by the Benedictine priory/cathedral. Probably the finest Norman building in the country, it survived the Dissolution by promptly ceasing monastic activities and converting to a secular cathedral. The Venerable Bede, the classic chronicler of early medieval times, is buried there, as is St Cuthbert, brought from **Lindisfarne**. Number 15 in the net income hierarchy, the priory had a gross income of £1,573 and a gross temporal income of £1,106 which could imply an estate of the order of 35-40,000 acres. The land lay between the Tyne and the Tees and by the Dissolution all was let, mostly on five to 15-year leases. The prior had the wisdom to appoint a monk to the position of Terrar, effectively a land agent, to manage the let lands. Like most other Houses, the welfare of the priory depended very much on the prosperity of the tenants who in turn depended on arable farming for their own livelihood, hobbled as many were by the restrictions of the manorial system. The monks did not stint themselves. Mid 15th-century accounts show purchases of sheep, cattle, pigs, fish, poultry, eggs, spices, cheese and butter. In one week, the priory consumed five cattle, 22 sheep, two calves, 13 piglets, a 'cart load' of fish, 22 hens and 400 eggs, not to mention bread, cheese, wine and beer. (I am indebted to R.D.Dobson for much of the foregoing.)

But the priory was not the only monastic House in the county. **Finchale** Priory (extensive ruins), just north-east of Durham city, was a small retreat for jaded monks from the big House, just as Thorney was for Peterborough monks in need of rest and recuperation. **Jarrow** was tiny, with an income of only £40 but big enough to sustain the most famous early medieval monk, the chronicler Bede.

Essex

At the Dissolution Essex had 19 religious houses. The smallest, each with a net income of £29 a year and owning little more than a large farm, were **Bernden**, seven miles north-west of Stanstead, and **Hedingham**, eight miles south-west of Sudbury. The largest was **Waltham Holy Cross**, the possible burial place of King Harold, killed at Hastings. An Augustinian abbey in Epping Forest, it had a net income of £900, suggesting around 30,000 acres. It was the last House to surrender, going down on 23 March 1540, thus ending over 900 years of monastic life as a major factor in English religious observance. Residual buildings are still in use as the parish church. **Colchester St Botolphs** was the first Augustinian House in England (founded 1095) but at the end had an income of little more than £100. There are substantial remnants of the buildings in the town centre. The splendid gatehouse of **St Osyth**, an Augustian priory close to Clacton, remains nearly intact. The priory had a net income of £677 and perhaps 20-25,000 acres.

Gloucester

There were three major Houses, **Gloucester St Peter's**, **Tewkesbury** and **Cirencester**. St Peter's was wealthy, with some 50 manors including the now very fashionable Cotswold villages of Northleach, Eastleach, Coln St Aldwyn, Down Ampney and Ampney St Peter. The abbey had built up a holding of perhaps some 50,000 acres at an average rent of around 7d./acre but was nevertheless living beyond its means. At the Dissolution/re-Foundation the House had creditors of £404. There were debts of £150 but the abbey did not seem very good at collecting them – Wm Cockes owed £20 for cattle bought from the abbot and other farmers were in arrears on £40. Residency at St Peter's also seemed generous. There were 30 monks living in along with three times this number of laymen. As an indication of monastic extravagance, the Commissioners found that the 30 monks had 86 servants. Tewkesbury was a little smaller with perhaps around 35,000 acres. Tewkesbury also had the extraordinary ratio of 39 resident monks to 144 live-in laymen. With this many mouths to feed, an unpaid bill for fish of £36 is perhaps not surprising. The abbey church survives in lovely order, as a continuing place of worship. The Augustinian abbey of Cirencester, about on a par with Tewkesbury on total wealth, nevertheless had some very poor land. Thin Cotswold brash was rented at no more than 1-2d/acre, about the lowest arable rent found. The land would have been better grassed down for sheep but perhaps the tenantry needed the ground for basic food crops. The abbey site is now occupied by a block of flats.

HAMPSHIRE

Monastically dominated by **Winchester**. The Benedictine priory converted to a cathedral at the Dissolution, becoming the longest church in England as Glastonbury was demolished. It had then some 45-50,000 acres, about number 14 in the monastic landowning hierarchy. In earlier years, the monastery had been a leader in agricultural development. At the end of the 13th century, there were 13,000 acres of arable land in hand, 30,000 sheep and 3,500 cattle. The abbey re-invested sufficient of its income at least to maintain its estates. A barn built in 1310 at Ivinghoe, Bucks., a major Winchester estate, for £83 8s. was still in use at the Dissolution. The abbey kept detailed records of the construction - 63,500 nails for the barn cost 9d. per 1,000 and food for the workers 23s. **Hyde** or New Minster built to the north of the Cathedral was quite wealthy, perhaps with 25-30,000 acres. It was most effectively demolished within a year or so of Dissolution by Thomas Wriothesley, later Earl of Southampton, colluding with Thomas Cromwell who shared in the spoils. Wriothesley survived to become Lord Chancellor. Cromwell, undermined by the Duke of Norfolk, did not. All his massive acquisitions reverted to the Crown by attainder on his execution. Wriothesley retained some of the richest manors including Letcombe, where Waitrose now run a large organic farming business.

Beaulieu was a Cistercian house, the site of which is now the National Motor Museum. Originally founded by King John (not all bad) at Faringdon, Berkshire, it was rapidly moved to Hampshire on new land donated by John. Together, the estates probably totalled around 10,000 acres. The abbey hung on to the Faringdon land although well beyond the approved distance from the new Mother-house. Fertile meadow land in the Meon valley was also acquired to augment summer grazing and winter hay supplies. The marvellous barn at Great Coxwell (National Trust) built on the abbey grange at Faringdon in the early 1300s speaks eloquently of the abbey's activities and is an even better example of monastic investment than Ivinghoe.

Romsey, a well endowed Benedictine nunnery, survives to the extent of the splendid abbey church, now the parish church. The value of the estate is debatable and at the end seems to have involved some insider dealings. Sir Thomas Seymour, then on the inner circle of Royal favour, gained the abbey's land in Hampshire and Wiltshire, probably all it had. The Court of Augmentations recorded a gift to Sir Thomas on 23 March 1538 worth annually £251, a generous present which could have had a capital value of £5,000 and represented perhaps 10,000 acres or more. In typical Tudor court fashion, the gift did Sir Thomas little good. He was executed for treason on the orders of his brother, the Lord Protector, after Henry VIII's death. The future Queen Elizabeth I described him as a man of much wit but little judgment.

HEREFORD

Abbey Dore, this lovely relic of religious life (part of the original abbey is still in use as a parish church), had a stormy early life with feuding neighbours disputing forcibly the abbey's property even to the extent of kidnapping monks and being very beastly to them – hanging them upside down on alternate days. While nine of the abbey's 17 granges lay in England, the rest were across the border in Wales and this was a cause of the territorial troubles. An early member of the conservation movement, Gerald of Wales, accused the monks of wholesale clearance of woodland 'changing an oak wood into a wheat field'. But he later admitted the monks' shrewdness when the timber was sold for three times the cost of clearing. The abbey, beautifully situated in the Golden Valley, had a reputation for getting the top price for 'the finest wool in England' according to Francis Pegolotti , the Italian merchant with whom **Rievaulx** and **Fountains** got into serious debt. He priced the Lemster Ore (Leominster Gold) at £13 per sack against Lindsey (Lincoln) at £6. At the Dissolution, the abbey had 560 acres of demesne including 400 acres of arable, water mills and the usual collection of sheep houses, ox byres and dovecotes. There was only a gross income of £87 and temporal income of £66 and was but a modest landowner with perhaps 2,000-2,500 acres in all. Sir John Scudamore, whose ancestors had been among the early despoilers, paid £379 for the abbey and perhaps 800 acres out of a possible 2,500 which the abbey may have owned. He also bought the farming livestock and deadstock as a going concern. The family later made amends for their ancestors' activities by restoring the church in the 1630s. **Wigmore** was the major House in the county in money terms (gross income £317). Ruins survived to be used as a film set by John Challis, best known for his role in 'Only Fools and Horses. The demesne comprised 144 acres arable at 3d./acre, 64 acres of pasture at 17d. and 54 acres meadow at 21d. The total holding was of the order of 5-6,000 acres.

HERTFORD

The monastery of note was **St Albans**, the fourth or fifth largest House after Glastonbury, Canterbury, Westminster and, it seems, York St Mary's with a net income of £2,102. Founded in Saxon times in memory of Alban, the first English Christian martyr, the abbey grew in importance being near to London and on the main route north. Mathew Paris, c.1250, says the abbey stable had stalls for three hundred horses.

Property probably included some 60-70,000 acres but from a high at the turn of the 13th century, the abbey went downhill and was surrendered on 5 December 1539 by Abbot Boreman, installed solely for that purpose as the abbey affairs were a mess. In 1846, a barrister from Gray's Inn, Henry Hewlett, translated all the charters of the abbey from King Offa 793 (purporting to gift 50 habitations with cornfields, meadows, feedings and woods) up to King Edward IV (1484) confirming previous charters. The immensely repetitive documents show the length to which the monks went to establish title to their land, liberties and privileges. All properties were named but only in one case were acreages mentioned. This was to confirm that,

> I Henry by the grace of God, King of England, Duke of Normandy and Aquitane and Earl of Anjou … have confirmed to the Abbey of Saint Alban and the monks there serving God all the purchases which Monk Adam the cellarer obtained … 500 acres at Bigrove … 40 acres of land and one acre of meadow at Rothampstead etc.

The King's sign was witnessed at Winchester by many grandees including the Archbishop of Rouen and the Bishops of Winchester and Coventry.

The Hospitaller /Templar estates in Hertford included land sufficient to justify the founding of the market town of Baldock. (See page 15.)

HUNTINGDON

The county was dominated by **Ramsey** Abbey, a Benedictine House, seventh biggest in the country, which held around 45-50,000 acres. All that is left now is a magnificent gatehouse. Sir Richard Williams, a courtier and nephew of Thomas Cromwell, was quick off the mark to purchase the property at a bargain price of £4,963 4s. 2d. before his uncle's fall from grace and execution in July 1540. Due no doubt to its proximity

24 *Ramsey Abbey was in the top ten of the wealth league and probably held some 50-60,000 acres, much of it fertile fenland. The gate house above is all that remains. (David Ross.)*

to the rich waters of the fens, Ramsey had the highest fishery income traced of any monastery – £26 17s. 6d. annually. In the mid 15th-century, the monks of Ramsey were none too keen on the discipline of their order. Bishop Alnwick, after a visitation, chided the monks for taking fields for private gain, sowing woad and other crops, missing divine service and 'out of their liking', hiring women of ill fame to do the field work.

KENT

Now the leading church of the worldwide Anglican communion, the site of **Canterbury Christchurch** has been a place of worship since mid-Saxon times. After Glastonbury, it was the second richest monastery by net income (£2,433). Henry VIII commanded that it become a secular cathedral and so it happened with the 'popish relics' of Thomas a Becket removed on his orders. With land mainly in Kent but also in Norfolk, Suffolk, Oxford, Bucks, Essex, Surrey and Sussex, the priory estates will have required expert management. At the turn of the 13th century, this was provided by Prior Henry of Eastry, a leading agriculturist of his day perhaps more comfortable with appraising cheeses or the bushel weight of wheat than the Opus Dei. He probably had as much as 70-80,000 acres under his care and was responsible for drainage on Romney Marsh and at Sheppey. At the Valor Ecclesiasticus, it seems hard that the King's Commissioners did not accept that the cost of visiting the outlying estates were a legitimate cost which should be excluded from the tenth tax (10 per cent of the rental due to the Crown). But, perhaps like any comparable authority, they were on their guard against fiddled expenses. Sir Christopher Hales and his brother were stewards of the abbey at the dissolution. They were also purchasers of ex-monastic land to the extent of perhaps 5,000 acres – again people on the inside track.

Prior Henry may well have given friendly advice to the nuns of **Sheppey Abbey** on the management of their, say, 4,000 acres.

The Benedictine priory of **Rochester** was the second biggest monastery in Kent with perhaps 16,000 acres and could have been the biggest – St Augustine's monks moved there from Canterbury in the seventh century but later moved back. The Norman abbey church survives.

LANCASHIRE

A fairly modest Cistercian Abbey, Whalley lies some six miles north-east of Blackburn. It held perhaps less than 10,000 acres and at the suppression could only show 84 horned cattle, 160 sheep, 10 pigs and 12 working horses. Perhaps they had given the rest away, for Whalley was notable for the extent of its charitable giving. At £121 18s. 10d. this was more than Westminster and only a little less than Glastonbury (£145 16s. 8d.). The general run of monastic charity was about 3 per cent of gross income. If the Valor Ecclesiasticus data is correct Whalley gave away 23 per cent of gross income. This charitable giving was noted in the Valor Ecclesiasticus and approved by the Commissioners (usually very strict on this) as being free of the Tenth, the standard 10 per cent Government tax on monastic income. A further indication of the charitable attitude of the Whalley monks was the provision of corrodians: free board and lodging at the Abbey. This could be obtained by purchase, earned by good works, established as founders rights or offered to the deserving poor. Whalley had 24 such poor residents, Westminster but 18 and many houses none at all. Whalley was often at odds with its Cistercian sister at **Sawley** (missed by Prof. Savine), a few miles to the north over property matters and tithes. As members of the same order, why could they not live at peace?

However, on one matter they seemed level pegging as potential entrants to the 16th-century Lancashire Good Loo Guide. At Sawley, the reredorter or necessarium channel can be clearly seen amongst the ruins. At Whalley, the necessarium was directly above the River Calder. Such matters were very important for the monks in every monastery, but could cause concern downstream. Suspected of complicity in the Lincolnshire Rising, the last Whalley Abbot, Father Paslew, was hanged, the property confiscated by the Crown and the monks turned out to other Houses.

Now, the abbey site with a well preserved gatehouse is a Church of England retreat in a lovely garden setting, open to the public and with excellent conveniences.

Leicestershire

The largest house was Augustinian **St Mary's Leicester**, with perhaps 20-25,000 acres. All the land was in the county apart from two manors in Lancashire. The holdings included Stoughton, the one-time headquarters of the Co-op UK farming operations now sold to the Wellcome Trust. At the Dissolution, the demesne was still being run on the three-field system but the monks had managed to enclose their grassland so they could control and manage the grazing. **Croxton**, the second largest monastery, was run by the Premonstratensian order, a stricter version of the Cistercians. Situated some five miles south of Belvoir, south-west of Grantham, no ruins remain above ground but the site was assessed in 1926 for the Duke of Rutland on whose land the abbey site lay. It was, however, well documented in the 16th century. There were 711 acres of demesne out of a possible 10,000 acres overall. The King's Commissioners for the suppression of the abbey, Robert Burgoyne and George Gifford, reported that at the site there were:

> orchards, gardens, stables, barn, dovecote and other houses meet for a farmer with one water mill.

Though mostly in Leicestershire, estates were scattered through Lincolnshire, Nottingham, Lancashire, Yorkshire with a tiny holding in Huntingdon worth no more than 9s. a year.

Lincolnshire

Second only to Yorkshire in the number of Houses, 51 against 67. Nevertheless, there are few monastic remains. The north of the county took the lead in the rebellion of 1536, the only serious opposition to the nationalisation of the monastic estate. Henry VIII took his revenge. Many executions were the result, with rapid demolition of almost all monastic buildings. An exception was **Crowland** in the south-west of the county. It has well preserved monastic remnants and part is still in use as the parish church. With a net income of £947, it was also the richest House in the county and may have had 30,000 acres. Much of the history of Crowland relates to feuding, often vicious, with neighbouring **Spalding** (net income £766). The marshlands controlled by Crowland were 'a veritable paradise providing wood for fires, fodder for cattle, thatch for roofs and birds and fish for food'. Spalding wanted a share of this but the territorial battles between two Benedictine houses were unseemly to say the least. There is nothing to show for **Revesby** now except a stone in a bumpy pasture field locating the position of the high altar. It may have owned 10,000 acres and had a stone quarry bringing in £6 11s. a year. It was a Cistercian daughter House of Rievaulx. The Valor actually gave limited information on field names, acres and rent. The author has walked these fields with such names as Thistle Close, Ten Acre Close and The Wong (Danelaw term for an enclosed often marshy area). The rents then were 7d./acre, now say £70/acre. In turn, Revesby monks established another daughter House at Cleeve in Somerset – very well preserved buildings – a pleasure to visit. **Sempringham**, north of Bourne, was the home of the only exclusively English monastic House. Founded in 1311 by Gilbert of Sempringham, it was unique in providing for both monks and nuns in the same community. Sort of. Though they were not allowed to meet socially, they could share in the church singing provided they could not see each other. Other Gilbertine Houses in the county were **Alvingham**, **Bollington**, **Cattley**, **Haverholme**, **Lincoln St Catherine's**, **Nunormesby** and **Sixhills**. Together they probably had about 25,000 acres in the county. In earlier years, the Templar Knights had major holdings in the county, particularly in Lindsey. Most of this land went to the Hospitallers when the Templars were forcibly disbanded.

LONDON AND MIDDLESEX

Westminster was the third richest abbey on net income, second on gross temporal income and the second largest landowner. Glastonbury was top on all three counts. Edward the Confessor established Westminster at the centre of English national life and William the Conqueror followed in this, as has been the case ever since. The abbey received endowments of land in Anglo-Saxon times, particularly from Edward the Confessor. These included land at Kelvedon in Essex and Brickendon in Hertfordshire as well as in Worcester and Gloucester – Pershore and Deerhurst with a thriving vineyard. Forty years before Domesday Book, the abbey held land in Hertfordshire, Essex, Surrey and Middlesex including the manors of Paddington and Hampstead. After the Conquest, William wished to 'afforest' Windsor Great Park but not against the wishes of the monks of Westminster to whom it had been given by Edward the Confessor. In exchange for giving up Windsor to the Crown (with whom it has remained ever since, probably the longest unbroken title in the country) the monks gained Battersea and Wandsworth in London and Feering and Ockenden in Essex. In financial terms the monks probably got the better deal. Though the figures can only be conjectural, Westminster probably had between 70 and 80,000 acres under ownership or control. This land comprised 110 separate estates in 19 counties.

The well connected nuns of **Bridgettine Syon** had perhaps 40,000 acres including land in Devon. This was to support their take over of St Michael's Mount in Cornwall from the French mother house.

The **Knights of St John of Jerusalem (Hospitallers)** were based in London but were an Order rather than a House. They may have had as much as 40-45,000 acres registered in London in addition to the land noted in the county returns, but this is open to doubt. They were given much of the Templars' land when that order was forcibly dissolved in 1312 because their financial and military strength was an embarrassment to the 'authorities'.

NORFOLK

The county was well supplied with religious Houses – 33 in all. The biggest (net income £871) was the Benedictine **Norwich Cathedral Priory** with the largest and best surviving cloister in the country and the second highest spire after Salisbury. Nifty negotiations, that is to say a humble petition to the King and his council to convert the monastery to an Anglican cathedral, succeeded, thus avoiding the demolition of the building. The Prior, William Castleton and 21 monks became, at the stroke of a quill on 2 May 1538, a Dean, prebendaries and canons whose duty it was to serve God and pray for the King and his ancestors. Norwich was the first of several monasteries to survive to the present day in this way. The Priory's property, which probably included more than 20,000 acres, was transferred to the new Dean and Chapter. Almost all the estates were in Norfolk, the largest at Martham and Sedgeford, each thought to have about 2,000 acres. The smallest, Thornham, now part of 'Chelsea by the Sea', barely 300.

On the somewhat flimsy pretext of a Saxon lady's vision of the Virgin Mary in 1061, the Augustinian monks of **Walsingham Priory** built themselves into the second richest House in Norfolk. Nearly half their income came from 'spiritual' giving and dues but they may well have accumulated over 10,000 acres as well. In spite of Henry VIII making a pilgrimage there in 1513, the monastery, after a somewhat scandalous past, was willingly surrendered by Prior Vowell in 1538. He helped in the destruction and received a pension of £100 a year. His deputy objected and was hanged for his opinions.

Castle Acre. This was a Cluniac priory of which there were 32, mostly modest, Houses in England. It is included here because of the wonderful ruins which remain. The prior's lodgings are almost as he left them. The net income was £307 and there was probably around 5,000 acres to support a fashionable monastery.

NORTHAMPTONSHIRE

At the time of the Dissolution, the ancient Soke of Peterborough was in with Northampton. It therefore appears now under that county. **Peterborough Abbey**, ninth richest in the country in 1540 with a net income of £1,722, was founded in 653 and the foundation survived to become the wonderful cathedral it now is. The uniquely beautiful west front is marred only by the later addition of the completely inappropriate porch. The initial massive early medieval grant to Medeshamstede (Peterborough) was described earlier. It could have been as much as 100,000 acres. A description of Peterborough monastic farming appeared on page 19 *et seq*. At the dissolution, the abbey had an estimated 60,000 acres by which time the land was almost all let.

But Peterborough was only one of 13 religious houses in Northampton. **Catesby** was a small (4-5,000 acre) nunnery south-west of Daventry. It was run shrewdly by Benedictine ladies on their demesne of 1,032 acres. 161 acres of arable were valued at 6d./acre, 788 acres pasture at 15d. and 83 acres meadow at 20d. The whole demesne averaged 14d./acre. Most of the grassland was enclosed and the Dissolution Commissioners found 1,124 sheep, value £200 and 110 cows and bulls, value £96. The nuns had been honest and not sold off their stock as other Houses had done. The demesne income from mostly enclosed land was three times that from the customary tenants, due no doubt to the inefficiencies of the strip system imposed on the customaries. The nuns seem to have achieved a good stocking rate for their livestock of around three acres per cattle beast or sheep equivalent.

NORTHUMBERLAND

Perhaps the smallest of all Benedictine Houses was that on the Farne Islands. Windswept and lonely, the Commissioners put no more than £12 as the annual value of the islands where St Cuthbert had lived most of his life as a hermit and died there in 687. Seven miles to the north, the romantic **Lindisfarne**, accessible at low tide by a causeway, was valued at four times as much. Temporarily the resting place of St Cuthbert (permanent home in Durham Cathedral) and now a major nature reserve, Lindisfarne monks produced the incomparable illuminated Lindisfarne Gospels now in the British Library.

From piety to practicalities, the largest monastery in Northumberland was **Tynemouth** built inside a Norman fortress. Attacks from the Scots were a continuing if reciprocal hazard to all Border monasteries. With a net income of £397, the monastery may have had some 13,000 often strife-torn acres to support it. **Hulne**, a Carmelite priory, escaped the eagle eye of the commissioners, inasmuch as it does not seem to figure in the Valor Ecclesiasticus, possibly because it was tucked away deep in the private Percy park north of Alnwick Castle. It can be visited with permission from the Alnwick Estate Office and has been described as 'Arcadian'. In the same park to the south stands just the impressive gatehouse of **Alnwick Abbey**. This was given a Valor Ecclesiasticus net income of £189 and presumably absorbed into the Percy estates. **Hexham Abbey** with perhaps 4,000 acres is now the parish church but retains two noteworthy structures. The Anglo-Saxon crypt is the best preserved in the country and the Night Stair brings home the reality of sleep be-fuddled monks struggling down from their dormitory into the abbey church to attend matins at 2am and then lauds at 4am on a cold winter's morning. Were they early hoodies, pulling their habits and hoods around themselves in a vain effort to keep warm?

NOTTINGHAMSHIRE

Nottingham County Council have made a good job of **Rufford** Abbey. It now provides a 'Great Day Out for all the Family' two miles south of Ollerton. Matters were not so good around 500 years ago. The abbey, in the heart of Robin Hood Country (if that ever existed!), was in trouble, falling numbers and scarce resources meant poverty and so Rufford was one of the first houses to surrender, which it did in 1536. Even so, the commissioners still gave it a value of £186 representing perhaps 6,000 acres. Unusually, the monks had been accepting a considerable proportion of their rents in kind: wheat, barley, oats, rye and peas. Perhaps the grain was not delivered in a timely fashion or was not up to standard. Rufford was a Cistercian house and in earlier years the monks had had a reputation for clearing the (Sherwood) forest, selling the timber and grazing sheep on the reclaimed land. The vandals! – desecrating 'ancient woodland'! After suppression, the estate was given to George Talbot, 4th Earl of Shrewsbury, along with other land. He was lucky to be among the early beneficiaries of gifted land. In later years, most had to pay the full price of 20 years' purchase on the rent.

The sale of the assets of the Premonstratensian **Welbeck** Abbey helped to lay the foundation of a future massive landed estate, that of the Dukes of Portland.

25   *Lindisfarne – Holy Island – Insula Sacra. Yes, in the early days Lindisfarne was indeed a cradle of Christianity with St Cuthbert's occupancy of the island, a practical church and devout monks who produced the Lindisfarne Gospels, beautiful 7th-century illuminated scripts now in the British Museum. All that changed with the Norman Conquest. A Benedictine monastery was established under William of Calais with endowments on the mainland. The Almighty held sway for some while but gradually gave way to Mammon. The monastery became the centre of a substantial commercial operation and the few monks involved lived very well – sugar, spices, almonds, olive oil and ginger appeared in the later accounts. There were also pickings from ships unfortunate enough to get wrecked on the island. The 'Rainbow Arch' was part of the Norman building financed by assets on the mainland which included over 1,000 acres of land as well as trading and investments.*

In 1883, the family were in the top ten with 64,000 acres. They still have some 17,000 acres, 4,000 farmed in hand. At the dissolution, the abbey site was sold to Richard Whalley, possibly a London Clothier, in February 1539 for £500. The landed income was around £165 which suggests an estate of some 5,500 acres. With the abbey site went perhaps 1,000 acres. He bought at 20 years' purchase i.e. an annual rent of £25 and made a further (joint) purchase in July 1545 for £197 – perhaps 400 acres. Mr. Whalley sold on to the 7th Earl of Shrewsbury for £555 in 1599 who in turn sold to the Newcastle /Cavendish connection from whom it passed by inheritance to the Dukes of Portland and became their principal home, an enormous mansion still called Welbeck Abbey, occupied by family descendants but bearing no relationship to the original Premonstratensian abbey of 1540. The last abbot, Richard Bentley, surrendered gracefully in 1538 with a pension of £50.

The wealthiest Nottingham House was **Thurgarton** Priory with less history attached and some 6-7,000 acres. Remains of the abbey church, including a splendid west tower, are in use as the parish church. Other houses of note were **Newstead** Priory now abbey and an imposing private house with connections to the family of Lord Byron, and **Worksop** Priory with a lovely gatehouse remaining.

OXFORD

The monastic life of the county was not very obvious. Perhaps the religious zeal went to the University. The 13 houses were noteworthy neither for their piety nor infamy. The largest was the Augustinian **Oseney** with some 20,000 acres. Second was **Eynsham** with perhaps 14,000 acres and one of the smallest **Goring**, an Augustinian nunnery with barely 1,000 acres to live off. **Dorchester**, a modest Augustinian abbey, survives in part as the parish church. **Christ Church** previously **St Frideswide's** enjoyed the protection of Henry VIII and prospered as Christ Church with monastic money.

SHROPSHIRE

The county was not a major player in monastic terms. The smallest of all, **Brewood**, a Cistercian nunnery, had a total income of £31 and a disposal income of only £18. Cistercian **Buildwas** (front cover) had 4-5,000 acres. Benedictine **Shrewsbury** was the wealthiest House with a total income of £559 and a disposable income of £483. The abbey had perhaps 15,000 acres. Little remains but the Norman nave is incorporated into the parish church. Two houses which still have plenty to show are **Wenlock** and **Haughmond**. Wenlock was a Cluniac House established in 1080 by Robert Montgomery, a principal adviser to King William, with monks from La Charitie-sur-Loire. Numbers built up to around 40 and remained fairly constant up to the Dissolution. The abbey may have had 10-11,000 acres but Cluniacs generally came to prefer to pay others to work their land rather than soil their hands with toil. This was not the original idea of the founders. Administration was not always up to scratch either. Colin Platt says in his book, *Abbeys & Priories of England*, that an Official Visitor from Cluny reported that the community was deep in debt in 1279 and that it was impossible to elicit the truth from the English monks. Along with Wenlock, Haughmond has extensive and even romantic ruins. A little smaller than Wenlock, it nevertheless probably held some 7-8,000 acres. One of the Stewards of Haughmond was the Earl of Shrewsbury, not you might think unusual but Professor Savine, the doyen of 20th-century analysts of the Valor Ecclesiasticus (the geld book of dissolution finance), considered that the Earl abused his position by holding ten such stewardships. These brought him fees of £35 a year as well as enabling him to have excellent insider information at the dissolution. In fact, George Talbot, 4th Earl of Shrewsbury, was Lord Steward of the Royal Household between 1509 and 1538 and was therefore ideally suited to seek and obtain a gift of land worth £246 in October 1537 and another worth £14 in June of the following year, perhaps as a leaving present. This could have involved in all some 9,000 acres of ex-monastic land. His successor, Francis, the 5th Earl, did a deal with the Court of Augmentations in November 1541 involving an exchange of land under which he received £485 from the Court perhaps in exchange for about 17,000 acres, if the rents were, say, 7d./acre – an average around that time. He re-invested £236 of this money in a purchase from the Court in 1545 of perhaps 8,000 acres, if the same figures are applied. All in all, the family may have ended up with about the same acres as they had before but with £500 'in the bank', equivalent to perhaps about 16,000 acres. High finance in the Tudor court of the time. A 16,000-acre deal on such land today (2014) would be likely to involve close to £100m.

Somerset

The county, and the whole national monastic estate, was dominated by **Glastonbury**. It was the largest landowner and the richest House, surpassing even Westminster in both these measures: 130,000 acres against Westminster 's estimated 75-85,000 acres and £3,312 net income against Westminster £2,409. The vast scale of the abbey church is obvious from the ruins (see page vi). It is the only House for which an accurate record exists of the total land held and the rents paid. This derives from a translation of Abbot Beer's terrier of 1516 carried out on behalf of the author. The terrier was compiled by Brother Thomas Sutton, the Outside Cellarer. Judging by his command of detail, he was a very competent land agent for the 130,000 acres held by the abbey.

The King was determined to get his hands on this asset which included a wealth of gold, silver and jewels in addition to the land. He did this by accusing the elderly Abbot Whiting of treason and hiding abbey assets. He had the poor man cruelly removed from this world through what was no less than a judicial killing. The King then got the assets with no further trouble. Some were passed to Queen Katherine Howard who had only temporary enjoyment of them. She was beheaded for alleged treason in February 1542 and the land returned to Henry VIII for disposal at his pleasure.

Glastonbury estates ranged through Somerset, Wiltshire and Dorset with outlying holdings in Berkshire and Devon (Uplyme). (More detail on Glastonbury may be found in *The Wealth and Estates of Glastonbury Abbey* published by the author in 2003.) The abbey was big business and activities included milling, fulling (wool), quarrying, bread ovens and brewing as well as slaughtering and tanning. Tithes were a major source of income as they were for most monasteries but not all went as far as the man in charge of the Brent manor (by the Sedgemoor Service Area) who, noting that one of the tenants had just had a tenth child, tried to claim the boy as a possession of the abbey!

Glastonbury was the origin of the nursery rhyme:

> Little Jack Horner sat in a corner,
> Eating his pudding and pie.
> He put in his thumb, pulled out a plumb and said
> 'What a good boy am I'

Sir John Horner was a lay official, bailiff of Mells and Steward of the Whitley Hundred, adviser to the abbey and responsible for land measurements – a professional surveyor. The Court of Augmentations shows a purchase by John and Thomas Horner on 10 July 1543 at 20 years' purchase in the sum of £1,831 19s. 11d. with an annual value of £76 3s. All above board and involved around 2,500 acres, almost certainly at Mells, their home base. However, it was recorded in 1539, that the parsonage

> ys in the Kynges gyfte and worth by the yere to farm £30 the vowson whereof is granted to Master Horner ut dic. (so they say).

It was the gift of the parsonage which will have given rise to the rhyme.

But Glastonbury was not the only abbey of significance in Somerset. There were 17 Houses of substance and five others with a net income of less than £60. **Cleeve**, near Watchet, probably had around 8,000 acres and was an interesting 1198 Cistercian spin-off from Rievaulx, Yorkshire via Revesby, Lincolnshire. The moves were made when both those Houses had more monks than facilities to accommodate them. The church has been demolished but the conventual buildings are among the best preserved in the country and a pleasure to be in, amongst the farm buildings. The gatehouse is also a memorable monastic relic. **Muchelney**, south of Langport, was the second largest house in Somerset and is also well worth a visit. The surviving abbot's parlour gives an idea of just how well the abbot of even a moderate House lived. He probably had around 12-13,000 acres to support his standard of living and, to a much lesser extent, that of his monks. At the Dissolution, the abbey and lands passed to Edward Seymour but reverted to the Crown on his later execution. A lot of monastic land came back to the Crown in this way. One of the biggest examples was Thomas Cromwell whose execution in 1540 meant that all his very considerable self-donated assets, say 50,000 acres, were available to the King for keeps or for his new best friends.

STAFFORDSHIRE

There were 12 houses for the 'religious'. The richest turned out to be Benedictine **Burton** on Trent by a wide margin after the office of the Chancellor of the Exchequer questioned the original Valor Ecclesiasticus valuation. An unusual occurrence and no doubt as a result of a tip-off. The net income was increased from £267 to £425. This might imply that there were 5,000 more acres than were valued in the first count making some 13,000 in all, or there was some other serious miscalculation or omitted assets. **Croxden**, a Cistercian abbey north-west of Uttoxeter, has some notable ruins but somewhat impaired by the road which cuts the site. The abbey was relatively modest with only about 3,000 acres but the monks worked hard on their demesne in hand, earning £37 a year according to the Valor Ecclesiasticus, a high figure for a small House. The Benedictine priory at **Tutbury** had perhaps 5,000 acres. A magnificent Norman doorway survived from the monastic church to be incorporated in the present parish church.

The story of **Dieulacres** is told at some length as it encapsulates much of the less attractive history of some medium-sized monasteries. It was a Cistercian abbey situated in rather bleak country north-west of Leek. In early years the abbot and monks had been accused of banditry and there were ongoing property disputes with Croxden which were, however, resolved. At the dissolution the incumbent abbot and his predecessor accused each other of issuing blank sealed charters, thus potentially allowing anyone into whose hands these came to claim what they liked. In 1538 there were then in residence the abbot, 12 other monks, 30 servants, eight poor bede women and 19 lay officials and sundry other persons. The abbey was surrendered in October that year and all got a pay off. The abbot and monks were granted pensions but these were slow to materialise and ex-Abbot Thomas Witney, living in Leek, was writing, in 1540, to John Scudamore (receiver at the Court of Augmentations and purchaser of the assets of Dore Abbey, Hereford) to ask for payment of overdue pensions for himself and his poor brethren, unable to work. However, the abbot lived another 18 years and was able to leave several bequests. The day after the surrender, the goods, furnishings and farm stock were sold to the Earl of Derby, the Steward of the abbey, for £63 14s. The abbey's debts were £172 and Lord Derby's money will have gone to offset these. The abbey assets were valued at £286 but these included appropriated churches and chapels and saltpans at Middlewich representing around 30 per cent of the total income. Removing these non-agricultural assets suggests a rural rental income of nearly £200 and an acreage of perhaps 6,000.

Suffolk

Bury St Edmunds was the lead House in Suffolk out of 18 and the 10th richest abbey in the country measured on net income. Bury had a substantial 'spiritual' income from its ownership of churches, tithes and jurisdiction over perhaps a third of Suffolk. This source of income did not directly affect the extent of the abbey estates which may have been as much as 70,000 acres. The abbey was founded around 903 when the relics (in whatever state) of King, later St Edmund, foully murdered by the heathen host of marauding Danes in 869, were moved there from a little wooden chapel at Hoxne. The town then built up around this increasingly rich and prosperous abbey. There was at times a rackety and destructive relationship with the burghers of Bury. They deeply resented the abbot's near total control of local matters. Having his own prison to enforce his edicts did not improve relationships between town and mitre. His powers were legal and confirmed by William I as were his jurisdictions. These provided a very good source of income from the courts and markets. The townspeople showed their feeling particularly forcibly in 1327 when the abbey was ransacked and, according to a local affidavit, 100 horses, 120 oxen, 200 cows, 10,000 sheep and 300 pigs, worth £6,000 in all, were carried off. But the round numbers make the claim suspect. The power of the state came to the rescue of the abbey and its wealth and a fine of £140,000 was imposed on the town. However, in 1333 in the presence of the King, this was mitigated by a treaty which required the payment of 2,000 marks (£1,333) for 20 years. The two massive surviving gatehouses at Bury suggest more of a fortified castle than a house of religious and holy persons. However, relations did improve as time went on and finally, of course, the abbey lost out. Greene King, the brewers, are now the major influence in the town with their 'irresistible Abbot

26   *Bury St Edmunds gatehouse.*

Ale'. Who is to say that this is not an improvement?

There is no clear indication as to who acquired the very large land estates of the abbey. However, Thomas, Duke of Norfolk was Steward of the abbey. No doubt he had a big say in what happened to the abbey's broad acres and his supporters will have been the gainers. The site of the monastery, in the centre of the town, was considered worthless by the Commissioners – how different from today when such a town-centre site would be keenly sought. Bury was surprisingly gentle with its farm tenants in the matter of entry premiums or 'fines' charging only £21 15s. in the final year against Westminster £66. The nuns at Shaftesbury and Syon came top of this league levying the unfortunate successor tenants £134 and £135 just for seeking to follow their parents on the family holding. It may have been legal but does not seem fair.

Butley, just inland from Orford, was the second richest house in Suffolk with little now to show for it. There were probably around 8,000 acres, about the national average for the whole country. It had the dubious honour of having Thomas Cromwell (him again) as a steward. Poultry rents were documented in detail as to quality. How did the monks ensure that the capons and cockerels were fat enough and the eggs fresh enough? Evict or fine any tenant at fault? **Leiston**, east of Saxmundham, has comprehensive ruins in the care of English Heritage and a Lady Chapel still in religious use. It was a Premonstratensian abbey founded in 1365 and at the Dissolution may have had something over 5,000 acres. This all went to Charles Brandon, Duke of Suffolk along with a great deal of other land particularly in Lincolnshire. Charles Brandon was very much a chum of the King as well as being his brother-in-law. The farmhouse created in the ruins after the dissolution is now the home of the Pro Corda Music School and the abbey site is available for weddings and other events.

SURREY

An interesting county monastically and obviously far more rural than today. There were nine houses in all, with the very substantial net income of £4,070, far more than many larger counties. There were six Houses of substance and the smallest of these was **Waverley**, significant in monastic history. It was the first Cistercian House in England, founded in 1128 two miles south-east of Farnham where the patron, the Bishop of Winchester, already had a castle. Thus it was not established in a wilderness as was the past and future wont of this order but in quite comfortable surroundings. But the Cistercians did, of course, go on to found many Houses in out of the way places. The abbey was dissolved in 1536 and probably had around 5-6,000 acres. The ruins, in the care of English Heritage, are sufficient to give an idea of this trend-setting abbey.

The main players in the county wealth stakes were five Houses. Two were Benedictine abbeys, **Bermondsey** and **Chertsey**. The site of Benedictine Bermondsey Abbey is located between Abbey Street and Grange Walk, had the support of Kings William I and II and has been excavated. The abbey apparently had land in Leicester, Hertfordshire, Bucks, Gloucester, Somerset and Kent. Chertsey was initially founded in 666 with a grant to Abbot Erkenwald of 200 dwellings in a place called Thorpe. The donor was Frithwald, sub-Regulus of Surrey, and was perhaps the first obviously urban monastic gift. Most endowments were hides or carucates of land because that was what the donors were long on. Overall, probably less than 10 per cent of monastic assets could be classed as urban at the Dissolution. A little bit of the history of Chertsey has a modern ring to it. In the early 14th century, dispensation was sought for a monk, John de Winton who, with others, wounded a thief who had broken into the infirmary. The thief subsequently died of his injuries. The abbot, John de Rutherwyke, suspended monk John from divine service and sought counsel of the bishop who decided that, as it was not clear exactly how the thief had died, monk John should not be punished and be allowed to celebrate mass again. Only legitimate force had been used.

There were two Augustinian priories, **Merton** and **St Mary's Southwark**. Merton, the richest House in Surrey, was demolished in 1538 and the stone used for Henry VIII's palatial follies of Nonsuch and Oatlands. Southwark partially survived the Dissolution and became the parish church and subsequently Southwark Cathedral as it is today.

There was a Charterhouse at **Shene**, wealthy with a net income of £777, the second highest in Surrey. The Carthusian monks lived a particularly plain and solitary life there, coming together from their mini cottage cells only once a week for church. There was another Charterhouse in London and the one at Mount Grace in Yorkshire is very well preserved. It is odd that such a strict order should be best remembered for the green liqueur invented at Le Grande Chartreuse at the original site of the Order in France. When in 1519 Thomas Goulding was sent from the London Charterhouse to Mount Grace, it was said that he took with him a 'doubyll styll to make … aqua-vitae'. **Tandridge** and **Reigate** were two modest Augustinian priories and brought up the rear with only £61 temporal income apiece but still around 2,000 acres each to live off.

Sussex

Of the 11 Houses in the county, the Benedictine **Battle Abbey** was the richest and best known but it took a prod from the Pope to persuade William I to build it in memory of those killed at the Battle of Hastings, fought at Battle and not Hastings. Judging by the way he encouraged the slaughter of Saxons especially in the north of England, the only good Saxon would seem to have been a dead one as far as 'William the Bastard' was concerned. The memory of his own people killed, the strong wish to keep onside with God along with thankfulness for his victory were the forces driving the building which was not finished in his lifetime. The abbey probably accumulated some 25,000 acres and their activities included a tile works at Alciston worth £3 13s. 4d. a year and mills which brought in £10 13s. 4d. Whether all the land came with good title could be questioned. Claims of forgery were quite common in the monastic world but seem to have been alleged notably at Battle. They may have had a DIY Title Deed Kit to the greater glory of God, of course, but also to the benefit of the abbey's net worth. One can imagine Abbot de Grabbit quietly instructing Brother Ignoramus to go and 'search the archives for papers concerning the manor of Great Whatever which we are sure belonged to us in the time of King Englebert. And if you cannot find them you

27   *The gatehouse of Benedictine Battle Abbey, East Sussex. Started by William I as a war memorial for those Normans lost in 1066 but not finished in his lifetime.*

can surely remember and make a copy'. The Abbot could be fairly safe as few could read the documents and if better title could not be proved, the abbey would take over. Battle had 22 manors and all but one were let to 'farmers' some of whom were certainly 'gentlemen'. In this way, the words gradually came to take on their modern meaning. Battle Abbey is now a school but English Heritage organise access to the historic site.

Lewes was one of the leading Cluniac House in the country of which there were only 32; Castle Acre, Wenlock and Thetford are others with noticeable ruins. Lewes Priory had an impeccable start, being founded by William de Warenne, known to have been present and active at the Battle of Hastings and made Earl of Surrey as a reward. The priory was well endowed with land both in Sussex and elsewhere totalling some 18-20,000 acres. It was involved in plenty of political trouble in later years as it was an alien house controlled by the Abbot of Cluny in France. The priory was surrendered on 16 November 1537 and the site acquired by, yes, the controlling power behind the whole Dissolution, Thomas Cromwell. He arranged for the immediate professional demolition of the priory including much of the church which was the largest in Sussex. 1536-46 was a good decade for demolition contractors but at what a loss to England's architectural heritage. There are useful remains still to be seen at Lewes in spite of Cromwell's efforts.

Bayham Abbey and **Boxgrove** and **Michelham** priories are three smaller Sussex Houses worth a visit. Boxgrove is still in parochial use. Bayham and Michelham are romantic leftovers from the monastic era.

WARWICKSHIRE

19 houses the largest of which was **Coventry**, initially a Bendictine Priory and later a cathedral. There was a sound foundation in 1043. Leofric, Earl of Chester, and his famous wife Godiva endowed it with half the town and 24 lordships. The house had the usual ups and downs and at the Dissolution had a net income of £543 of which, unusually, a quarter was of urban origin. The house must have hung on to quite a lot of the half of the town they started with. The surrender in 1539 was a typical put-up job. The long-standing prior Thomas Wyford conveniently died in 1537 and a placeman, Thomas Carnswell, was put in for the express purpose of helping with the suppression. For this service he got the very substantial annual pension of £133 6s. 8d. The cathedral church and buildings were knocked down and the site sold in 1545 to John Combes and Richard Stansfield for £987 with an annual rental income of £139. These gentlemen must have been in favour as some of their acquisition was at seven years' purchase instead of the normal 20 years' purchase. Also in Coventry but at the opposite end of the religious and financial spectrum was the **Coventry Charterhouse**. The reclusive monks had a net temporal income of only £21, having presumably given away the rest of their £131 income. Whether they owned much land is not clear but they had succeeded in removing common rights from their demesne. They also had woods: six acres of seven-year woods worth £3 6s. 8d. when mature at 16 years and 1.5 acres of three-year wood. This will have been coppice, probably cut for little winter fires in their mini-cottage cells. Augustinian **Kenilworth**, second richest in the county, probably had 10-12,000 acres. The suppression accounts recorded arable demesne land as Priors felde 70 acres (16s. 8d.), Wyndmill felde 80 acres (16s. 8d.) and Furze felde 66 acres

(13s. 4d.) The three approximately equal fields suggests that the three-field system was still being practised at a rent of 2s. 6d./acre payable to the monks. The Prior's Hall survives as a museum of the history of the abbey. **Stoneleigh** was a modest Cistercian abbey with perhaps 5-6,000 acres. From the Dissolution accounts, it comes out as one of the most heavily indebted monasteries. Monies owed at £219 were greater than the year's net income of £151. Some of the debts were way overdue such as the money due to Cecil Higgins for cattle purchased seven years previously. There were 46 lay persons and only 12 monks living off the monastery's resources and they seemed to be a drunken lot as debts included £75 for malt over two years (equivalent to the annual rent from 2,500 acres). There was no excuse for not paying at least some of the debts as the abbey had plenty of timber: 328 acres under eight years; 60 acres over 14 years and 160 acres over 100 years worth nearly £400. At the Dissolution, the abbey assets went to Charles Brandon, Duke of Suffolk. He sold on to Sir Thomas Leigh whose heirs are still there. The parkland is best known today as the home of the Royal Agricultural Society of England.

WILTSHIRE

There were 15 Houses of which four were nunneries and three of these were well endowed. If a lady was taking the veil from conviction or family pressure, Wessex was not a bad area for choices with Shaftesbury just across in Dorset, Winchester St Mary's in Hampshire and three Houses in Wiltshire to choose from: Wilton, Amesbury and Lacock. **Wilton** was a Benedictine nunnery with close to 20,000 acres and a net income of £601. Domesday Book noted 231 hides in Wiltshire and 12 elsewhere. Like so many Houses, these nuns had continuing financial problems in spite of their wealth. They had problems funding the four or five Knights Service required by the state in the 13th century and probably disposed of land to rid themselves of this liability. They took quite a lot of their rents in kind: 45 tons of wheat, 57 tons of barley, 27 tons of oats, 62 capons, 110 hens, 105 geese, a calf and eight loads of hay as well as running their own sheep flock for which they would need the hay. They earned £21 from their demesne activities and £11 from timber sales. At the Dissolution, the abbey buildings were in poor repair and the site and lands were sold to Sir William Herbert. King Henry's Letters and Papers and the accounts of the Augmentations Court suggest that he had the lot and half possibly as a gift. In any case he acquired enough land to be made the Earl of Pembroke a little while later. Land was the essential requirement for earldoms in addition to the King's favour. The new Earl and his successors built Wilton House on the site of the old nunnery and the 18th Earl is now in occupation and opens the house to the public.

Amesbury. Another well-off priory convent. In earlier 15th-century years, the Pope had on at least three occasions granted absolution to nuns who had become pregnant but in the later years they appear to have kept their affairs in better order. At the Dissolution their only debt was £20 14s. for current provisions and the prioress was allowed to keep money collected from the abbey's debtors. They farmed out much of their demesne: 290 acres of arable earned 4d./acre, 15 acres of pasture 17d./acre and 31 acres of meadow 20d./acre. They kept their own sheep flock and had rights of common grazing at 1d./sheep for 374 ewes. The bulk of the assets went to Edward Seymour, later 1st Duke of Somerset and Lord Protector in the minority of

Henry VIII's son Edward VI. Somerset was later indicted for misuse of his powers and executed – a standard Tudor political procedure as noted elsewhere. Nothing remains of Amesbury Priory.

The opposite is true of **Lacock**. Much of this modest Augustinian nunnery remains intact. Three sides of the nuns' cloister survive in the care of the National Trust along with many other convent rooms. Founded by Ela, Countess of Salisbury in 1240, it became an elegant and aristocratic home for her and her unmarried female family and friends over several generations with daughters of the local gentry gradually being admitted. A most comprehensive dowry was provided for daughter Joan by her father Nicholas Sambourne when she took the veil in 1395. It included bedroom furniture, fur mantles and silverware.

Ela was not averse to pushing her luck in high places. Henry III granted her and the abbey a weekly cartload of wood from his forest at Melksham. She tried to have this provision upped to a cart load a day. The King declined but did give the abbey 40 acres of the forest to get their own wood as they willed. The manors were well spread and included Shorwell on the Isle of Wight. Management of this property must have absorbed much of its substance.

With the agreement of the local parson, the nuns succeeded in enclosing land in Lacock to mutual benefit of the abbey and the glebe. Much produce went directly to the abbey from the manors but supplies were also bought in quantity especially fish. The list reads like a top class fishmongers wares today – haddock, turbot, plaice, mackerel, hake, crabs, lobsters, salmon, oysters, lampreys, eels, bream, ray, ling and pollack. Herrings (salted) were too ordinary to mention and were often given as alms to the poor. The nuns owned a flock of 2,000 sheep at the beginning of the 16th century for which the customary tenants were required to do the hard work of foot trimming, lambing, washing and shearing. The flock, down to 600 at the Dissolution, was finally let 'to farm' with the manor of Chitterne along with all the other demesne lands. The whole estate, demesnes and customary, probably totalled 5-6,000 acres. At the suppression, no hint of scandal was disclosed, 'vertuous lyving' commended and although enquiry was made into the granting of long leases, none was revoked as improper. The abbey site and some 1,500 acres were sold to Sir William Sharrington in July 1540 for £783 at the full 20 years' purchase – 10s./acre capital value. The rest of the property was dispersed to a number of buyers.

The Benedictine abbey of **Malmesbury** was the richest Wiltshire House with maybe 25,000 acres. In Saxon times, the abbey had been quite a seat of learning. The monks seem to have run their affairs well, anyway from the Government's point of view. Sir William Petre, an Augmentations official who later bought land for himself, reported to Cromwell that there were 'much cattle, the shrine in good order and the demesne not let out to farmers'. However, the Valor Ecclesiasticus records that Edward Hungerford, gent, was renting 40 acres in the Cowfold at Quedelegy (Gloucs.) at 8d./acre, about the average for the whole abbey estate. At the Dissolution, there were 22 monks and 54 lay persons seeking a living from the net income of £798. The site along with about 3,000 acres was sold to a wool merchant, William Stumpe, in November 1544 for £1,518 and £70 10s. annual rent. He gave the residue of the church (much had collapsed) to the parish with whom it remains. The buildings were used to house looms and create employment for the town.

WORCESTERSHIRE

The county had 10 Houses of which four were nunneries. **Worcester Priory-**Cathedral was the leading house with a net income of £1,297. The peace and tranquillity apparent now was not always the norm but the priory started well with Wulfstan, later sanctified. He had the unique distinction of serving as prior/abbot at Worcester under the last two Saxon kings and the first two Norman ones. He made his number with the Conqueror and received two hides of land on condition that he 'intercedes faithfully for the conqueror's soul and for those who assisted him when he obtained the lordship of this land'. In view of William's record, it is difficult to know whether the prayers of even Wulfstan would get the Conqueror through the pearly gates. But it was on this sort of presumption that hundreds of thousands of acres were given to the monastic houses up to the 12th and 13th centuries. Later, it began to dawn on potential donors that monks' mumbled prayers might not after all be the best route to heaven. Worcester abbey lands, customs and privileges were also confirmed as part of King William's wish to keep on the right side of the Almighty. He may also have valued Wulfstan's insight into the Saxon mind. Richard I gave 614 acres of assarted land before going crusading. At the end, the priory probably had some 35,000 acres. The last prior, Henry Holbeach, was made Dean of the new cathedral in 1541. The priory was unusual in the high proportion of rent taken in kind. 60 tons of wheat, 50 tons of barley, six tons of rye, three tons of oats and some three tons of peas representing 10 per cent of the temporal income were recorded. Apart from the monks, their servants and the corrodians, the priory also fed 14 schoolboys, presumably with a view to their value as choirboys.

Only slightly smaller than Worcester was Benedictine **Evesham** with £1,138 net income. As with so many abbeys and priories, much time and money was spent on trips to Rome to persuade the Pope or his officials of the abbey's case against bishop or aristocrat – rather as now we have to go to Brussels to get permission for all sorts of things. Perhaps Chaucer's 'Canterbury Tales' gives some idea, on a very small scale, of how these monumental trips to Rome might have been accomplished. By the beginning of the 13th century, matters at Evesham seem generally to have been settled and Abbot Randulf could busy himself with improving the abbey lands, building mills and granges, fishponds and dovecotes, clearing forest and giving tenants the like right where cultivation seemed possible. At the Dissolution, some 30-35,000 acres were dispersed and all buildings demolished apart from the splendid bell tower still standing in the town centre. Proposals to establish a school in the abbey buildings were quashed by Thomas Cromwell and, in revenge, the townspeople apparently took what they could of the abbey substance.

Pershore was another substantial but rather smaller abbey, a Benedictine convent. The nuns' net income at the Dissolution was £640, virtually all from rural investments –only £3 11s. was recorded as urban. They may have had 18-20,000 acres. Woodland brought in £13 a year which suggests enough to keep the convent warm and maybe something left over to sell. Pre-conquest in 980, the evil Earl Alfhere of Mercia took by force some half of Evesham's land. Edward the Confessor did not help the local interest; he took back the land but gave it to Westminster Abbey, his continuing favourite. Pershore and Westminster remained cheek by jowl as local major landowners up to the Dissolution, with Westminster owning a dozen estates in the county. Early

14th-century Westminster rents ranged from 3d./acre to 8d./acre. The acreage can only be guessed at. However, if the evil Earl took half of Evesham's 980 assets which were then given to Westminster, the endowment might have been as much as 20,000 acres out of Westminster's 80,000 acres or thereabouts. To this day, the Dean and Chapter of Westminster are patrons of the Pershore living. The town bought the choir of the convent church for £400 and it remains a well buttressed, attractive but somewhat truncated parish church.

Yorkshire

This was the county with the largest and best known monastic spread – something like 300,000 acres out of a county total of 3.7m acres. There were 67 Houses of which the wealthiest was the Benedictine **St Mary's Abbey** in York with an annual income of close to £3,000 from all sources but records are not clear.

Fountains Abbey, near Ripon, is probably the best known of all English monastic sites. Set up by a break-away group of monks from St Mary's in 1132, they adopted the Cistercian rule and rapidly became very successful farmers with the aid of many lay brothers who did the work, while the full-time monks saw to the administration as well as the 'Opus Dei'. But by the end of the 13th century, farming affairs were in trouble due mainly to outbreaks of sheep scab. There was a debt to Italian wool merchants of £6,473 in 1291 and the abbey suffered the unique disgrace of having to mortgage the property to secure the debt to the lenders. It was bailed out by the government as too big to fail.

Around 1300, it was estimated that the monastery had at least 13,000 sheep producing not only wool, but sheep milk dairy products (for which there was an export trade) as well as skins and parchment. However, by the time of the suppression, sheep were down to 1,326 (the balance probably sold to the tenants as hefted flocks, born to their ground) but 2,356 cattle remained of which working oxen 536, cows 738, bulls 49 and the rest young stock. At the Dissolution. Fountains had a net income of £1,004 and a gross temporal income of £1,103. The abbey came to own substantial granges and the total land holding was probably of the order of 20,000 acres lowland plus 50,000 acres of moorland good only for sparse summer grazing. This land now comprises a major part of the Yorkshire Dales National Park between Wharfedale, Littondale and Ribblesdale and centred on Malham Tarn.

Fountains returned a very high income from its worked demesne – £183. But one suspects that little of this was due to the monks' own labour. A lot of paid workers probably produced this result. At the Dissolution the abbey site and about half the land by value was sold to Sir Richard Gresham, father of Sir Thomas, founder of the Royal Exchange in London for the massive figure of £11,138, the biggest sale recorded by the Court of Augmentations. This bought him some 10,000 acres of good land round the abbey as well as the 50,000 acres of moorland. A shrewd man, he persuaded the King to throw in a couple of nunneries as well. These were **Swyne** and **Nunkeeling** with 4,000 acres of excellent land round Beverley in the East Riding. The Gresham family were active buyers of land in later years – an early example of City money going into the country.

The Cistercian **Rievaulx Abbey** is interesting, often billed as a rich and successful abbey. However, apart from a flying start from Walter d'Espec with 1,000 acres of

28 *Fountains Abbey, near Ripon, Yorkshire is probably the best known monastery in the country but, at £1,004 net annual income, by no means the richest. It came 18th in the overall wealth stakes but was top of the Cistercian list. The ruins are impressive and the surviving cellarium unique in scale. The abbey held around 20,000 acres of low ground reasonably close to home but also extensive moorland of some 50,000 acres around and north of Malham tarn in the Yorkshire dales. The last years of the monastery saw unseemly feuding amongst those who had or wished to have the abbacy. Abbot Thryske, the incumbent was described, with little evidence, as a 'vera fole and a miserable ideote' by the Duke of Northumberland who was rooting for Marmaduke Bradley as the alternative. Bradley, described as an unscrupulous, ambitious man, got the job but was the last abbot, handing over to Cromwell's commissioners late in 1539 in return for an annual pension of £100. Poor Thryske was hanged in 1537 for alleged complicity in the 'pilgrimage of grace'. Such goings-on do not sit easily with the peace and tranquillity at Fountains today.*

arable land and the saintly Abbot Aelred, this is not borne out by the facts apart from the building activities. The structures have survived so well because it was too expensive for the demolition contractors to cart the stone away from such an isolated site. There was trouble with an overdue debt to Aaron of Lincoln in 1189 and a forward sale of their wool crop to Italian merchants in 1275 could not be delivered due to sheep scab. (Fountains had the same problem as noted above.) The resulting financial problems were so severe that there was talk of closing the monastery and possibly the abbey's finances were permanently weakened. At the

Dissolution, Rievaulx had only a net income of £279 and a disposable income of less than £200 which made it one of the first abbeys to be suppressed under the 1536 Act. The monks apparently 'went quyetly with no murmour of dissent', at least according to the Commissioners' report to Cromwell dated 15 December 1537 at York.

Post-Dissolution sales and gifts to the favoured soldier/courtier Thomas Manners, Earl of Rutland, an undoubted chum of the King, suggest that the majority if not all of the property ended up with Rutland. A the end of the 12th century as a rough estimate the abbey held some 6,500 acres grass, 2,500 arable and 3,000 other, totalling some 12,000 acres, possibly a little less at the Dissolution.

The Carthusian **Mount Grace** deserves a mention because it seems to be the only monastery which still had a waiting list of would-be monks at the beginning of the 16th century. Their continuing strict observance of The Rule, their isolation, and each occupied an individual mini-cottage cell with garden and they met only for church and spoke only when essential. No market there for pointless mobile phone chatter. These 20 or so reclusive folk had 9-10,000 acres to support their way of life. They did not give much away – 5s. (25p) was all the charitable giving they could manage in their final year. (See page 11.)

Byland, in an early morning mist, must be one of the more evocative monastic ruins anywhere in the country, lacking as it does the more commercial aspects of better known Houses. If a ruin can be beautiful, Byland is. The Cistercian monks who finally built this abbey had been nearly as peripatetic as the Israelites. They started in Cumbria at Furness, fell out in succession with four lots of religious colleagues with several attempts at Yorkshire homes before settling a few miles

29 *Byland. A Cistercian abbey of imposing proportions but only modest wealth. At £238, the net income was little more than one quarter of Fountains. However, out of these limited resources, probably no more than 7,000 acres, a great abbey complex was built. Our picture shows the north wall of the main church and the remains of an incredible rose window. John Alanbridge was the last abbot who surrendered with his 23 monks in December 1537. According to the records, they went "quyetly" and the commissioners "p'ceyved no mumure of grief" – the monks were relieved to be able to give up the unequal struggle involved in keeping the operation together.*

south-west of Rievaulx with whom there had been a serious campanological dispute. Byland along with Rievaulx, Kirkham and the very small Gilbertine House of Ellerton went down in December 1537 in the first round of the suppression of 'small houses sunk in sin'.

It seems that the Byland Abbey site and perhaps 2-2,500 acres out of a possible 7-8,000 acre total were sold to Sir William Pickering in September 1540 for £1,243 18s. 4d. Later, in March 1543, Leonard Beckwith took his first steps on the road to gentrification. He had been a commissioner for the suppression of a number of Yorkshire Houses and had prepared the detailed valuation on which Sir Richard Gresham made his massive Fountains related purchase, having his work formally checked 'Per nos Hugonem Fuller and Jacobum Rokeby, Audit'. Beckwith went on to buy for himself £505 12s.-worth of land, mostly it would appear ex-Byland assets and close to 1,000 acres. He later acquired a knighthood and was High Sheriff of Yorkshire in 1550.

Other notable Yorkshire Houses were, in size order, **Selby**, **Gisburn**, **Jervaulx**, **Bridlington** and **Whitby**. Whitby, wonderfully placed on the cliffs south of the town, had managed to get all its demesne enclosed – 66 acres of arable, 296 pasture and 30 acres meadow with an 18-acre close at an average rental of 12d./acre. Jervaulx and Bridlington were accused of aiding the Lincolnshire Rising. Their property was confiscated without compensation and the Abbots hanged. A cheap and easy way of getting the assets and not unique. Attainders were carried through when there was any excuse, as at Woburn and Glastonbury. The advantage to the King was that such assets came directly to him with 'no meddling', by-passing the Court of Augmentations.

A County List of all the Religious Houses noted in the Valor Ecclesiasticus

NOTES

The definitions of the Houses and Gross Temporal Income data have been taken from Prof. Savine's 1909 analysis of the Valor Ecclesiasticus: a = abbey, p = priory, n = nunnery, co = Commandary/Preceptory. A = Augustinian, B = Benedictine, C = Cistercian, Cl = Cluniac, Ch = Charterhouse (Carthusian), P = Premonstratensian, G = Gilbertine, Trin = Trinitarian, Fr = Franciscan, Bridg = Bridgettine, Bon = Bonhommes, Bethl = Bethlemites. The list is not exhaustive as certain properties are known to have been omitted from Prof. Savine's list. These appear in small type and have no estimate of income.

The Gross Temporal Income (GTI) has been reduced by 10 per cent to allow for non-agricultural income. Four counties (Berks, Cambs, Essex and Herts) had Net Income data only from the Liber Valorum. The NI has been reduced by 20 per cent for these counties. Two other counties (Hampshire and Northumberland) also had inadequate GTI data from the Valor Ecclesiasticus and have been treated in the same way. The estimates can only be approximate and may not exactly match other figures due to rounding and specific changes to the 6.5d. average rental estimate.

County	Gross Temporal Income less 10%	Estimated Acres generally at 6.5d/acre rent	County		
	£s			£s	acres
BEDFORD			BUCKINGHAMSHIRE		
Bushmead p A	74	2,700	Ankerwyke p B n	41	1,500
Caldwell p A	67	2,500	Bittlesden p C	117	4,300
Chicksands p B	183	6,800	Burnham a A n	65	2,400
Dunstable p A	310	11,400	Ivinghoe p B n	16	600
Elstow a B n	126	4,700	Lavenden a P	55	2,000
Harwood p A n	24	900	Little Marlow a B n	23	900
(Melchbo'rne co) p B n	49	1,800	Medmenham a A	16	600
Newnham p A	140	5,200	Missenden a A	179	6,600
Warden a C	370	13,700	Notley a A	159	5,900
Woburn a C	352	13,000	Snetteshall p B	22	800
BERKSHIRE			CAMBRIDGE		
Abingdon a B	1689	62,400	Anglesey p A	113	4,200
Bisham p A	257	9,500	Barnwell p A	231	8,500
Donnington p Trin.	18	700	Cantab. St.Edmund p G	14	500
Hurley p B	110	4,100	Chatteris p B n	87	3,200
Poughley p B	61	2,300	Denny a FR n	157	5,800
Reading a B	1745	64,400	Ely c p B	976	36,000
			Fordham p G	37	1,400

	£s	acres		£s	acres
Icklington p B n	64	2,400	**DORSET**		
Shengay co	158	5,800	Abbotsbury a B	353	13,000
Swaffham Bulbeck p B n	36	1,300	Bindon a C	167	6,100
Thorney a B	371	13,700	Cerne a B	504	18,600
			Cranbourne p B	19	700
CHESHIRE			Ford a C	335	12,400
Birkenhead p B	18	700	Holme p Cl	13	500
Chester St Mary p B n	67	2,500	Milton a B	529	19,500
Chester St Werbergh a B	676	25,000	Shaftesbury a B n	1090	40,200
Combermere a C	163	6,000	Sherborne a B	588	21,700
Norton a A	102	3,800	Tarrant a C n	196	7,200
Vale Royal a C	215	7,900			
			DURHAM		
CORNWALL			Durham c p B	995	36,800
Bodmin p A	195	7,200	Finchale p B	77	2,900
St Cyrus p Cl	9	300	Jarrow p B	19	700
St Germans p A	108	4,000	Wearmouth p B	8	300
Helston n secular ?	13	500			
Launceston p A	210	7,700	**ESSEX**		
Tywardreath p B	47	1,700	Barking B n	777	28,700
			Berden p A	26	1,000
CUMBERLAND			Beeleigh a P	142	5,300
Armthwaite p B n	12	400	Coggeshall a C	226	8,300
St. Bees p B	71	2,600	Colchester St Bot. p A	103	3,800
Calder a C	44	1,600	Colchester St Johns a B	472	17,400
Carlisle c p A	135	5,000	Colne p B	141	5,200
Furness a C	687	25,300	Dunmow p A	135	5,000
Holm Cultram a C	334	12,300	Hatfield Peverell p B	55	2,000
Lanercost p A	26	964	Hatfield Regis p B	111	4,100
Wetheral p B	52	1,900	Hedingham p B n	27	1,000
			Lees p A	103	3,800
DERBYSHIRE			St Osyth p A	609	22,500
Beauchief a P	69	2,600	Prittlewell p Cl	140	5,200
Breadsall p A	7	300	Stratford Langthorn a C	461	17,000
Dale a P	117	4,300	Thremhall p A	55	2,000
Darley a P	232	8,600	Tiltey a C	150	5,500
Derby Kings Mead p B n	17	600	Walden a B	336	12,400
Gresley p A	24	900	Waltham Holy Cross a A	810	29,900
Repingdon p A	66	2,400			
Yeveley & Barrow co	84	3,100	**GLOUCESTERSHIRE**		
			Cirencester a A	941	34,800
DEVON			Deerhurst p B	121	4,500
Barnstaple p Cl	103	3,800	Flaxley a C	101	3,700
Buckfastleigh a C	392	14,500	Gloucester St Oswalds p A	54	2,000
Buckland a C	193	7,100	Gloucester St Peter's a B	1327	49,000
Canonleigh a B n	149	5,500	Hayles a C	324	12,000
Carswell p Cl	24	900	Lantony p A	519	19,200
Cornworthy p A n	24	900	Stanley p B	38	1,400
Dunkeswell a C	261	9,600	Tewkesbury a B	952	35,200
Exeter St Nicholas p B	99	3,700	Winchcombe a B	639	23,600
Frithelstoke p A	69	2,600			
Hartland a A	135	5,000	**HAMPSHIRE**		
Newenham a C	189	7,000	Badersley co	107	4,000
Pilton p B	26	1,000	Beaulieu a C	293	10,800
Plymton p A	414	15,300	Bromere p A	140	5,200
Polslo p B n	89	3,300	Hyde a B	779	28,700
Tavistock a B	642	23,700	Netley a C	91	3,400
Tavistock p A	34	1,300	Mottisfont p A	112	4,100
Torre a P	242	8,900	Quarr a C (IoW)	121	4,500
Totnes p B	73	2,700	Romsey a B n	355	13,100
			Southampton St Denys p A	73	2,700

	£s	acres
Southwick p A	231	8,500
Titchfield a P	225	8,300
Twyneham p A	281	10,400
Wherwell a B n	305	11,300
Winchester St Mary a B n	161	5,900
Winchester c p B	1357	50,100
Wintney p C n	39	1,400
HEREFORD		
Abbey Dore a C	59	2,200
Aconbury p A n	46	1,700
Clifford p Cl	23	900
Flanesford p A	14	500
St Guthlac's p B	122	4,500
Lymbrook p A n	18	700
Wigmore a A	166	6,100
Wormesley p A	34	1,300
HERTFORDSHIRE		
St Albans a B	1892	69,900
Cheshunt p B n	12	400
Flamstead p B n	28	1,000
Hertford p B	66	2,400
Hitchin p G n	13	500
Redburn p B	8	300
Royston p A	81	3,000
Sopwell p B n	36	1,300
Wymondley p A	27	1,000
HUNTINGDON		
Hinchingbrook p B n	16	600
Huntingdon p A	114	4,200
St Ives p B	37	1,400
St Neots p B	174	6,400
Ramsey a B	1607	59,400
Sawtry a C	144	5,300
Stonely p A	32	1,200
KENT		
Bilsington p A	110	4,100
Boxley a C	176	6,500
Cant. St Augustine a B	1289	47,600
Canterbury c p B	2347	86,700
Cant. St Gregory p A	104	3,800
Cant. St Sepulchre p B n	30	1,100
Cumbwell p A	49	1,800
Dartford p A n	425	15,700
Dover p B	154	5,700
Dover St Radegund a P	92	3,400
Faversham a B	268	9,900
Folkestone p B	7	300
Horton p Cl	77	2,900
Langdon a P	50	1,900
Leeds p A	97	3,600
Malling a B n	176	6,500
Mutlinden p Trin.	48	1,800
Rochester p B	443	16,300
Sheppey St Sexberge a B n	104	3,800
Swinfield co	78	2,900
West Prekham co	57	2,100

	£s	acres
LANCASTER		
Burscough a P	50	1,900
Cartmell p A	75	2,800
Cockersand a C	166	6,100
Conishead p A	47	1,700
Furness a C	687	25,400
Holland p B n	11	400
Hornby p P	25	900
Lytham p B	39	1,400
Penwortham p B	27	1,000
(Sawley C)Whalley a C	251	9,300
LEICESTERSHIRE		
Bradley p A	18	700
Bredon p A	7	300
Croxton a P	287	10,600
Dalby & Rotheley co	208	7,700
Garendon a C	156	5,700
Grace Dieu p A n	84	3,100
Kirby Beller p A	110	4,100
Langley p B n	16	600
Launde p A	251	9,300
Leicester St Mary a A	660	24,400
Olverston a A	134	5,000
Ulverscroft p A	64	2,400
LINCOLNSHIRE		
Ailsham p A	55	2,000
Alvingham p G	90	3,300
Axholme Ch	157	5,800
Bardney a B	224	8,300
Barlings a P	242	8,900
Belvoir p B	54	2,000
Bollington p G	77	2,800
Bourne a A	99	3,700
Cattley p G	27	1,000
Crowland a B	818	30,200
Eagle co	112	4,100
Fosse p B n	5	200
Frieston p B	76	2,800
Goykwell p C n	14	500
Greenfield p C n	72	2,700
Grimsby p B n	9	300
Hagenby a P	85	3,100
Haverholme p G	62	2,300
Hevening p C n	25	900
Hirst p A	7	300
Humberstone a B	23	900
Irford p P n	10	400
Kirkstead a C	291	10,700
Kyme p A	77	2,900
Legbourne p C n	25	900
Lincoln St Cats. p G	111	4,100
Lincoln St Mary p B	16	600
Louth Park a C	131	4,900
Markby p A	115	4,300
Neubo a P	76	2,800
Newsome a P	67	2,500
Newstead p A	34	1,300
Nocton Park p A	41	1,500
Nuncotton p C n	38	1,400

	£s	acres		£s	acres
Nunormesby p G	67	2,500	Thetford p A	34	1,300
Revesby a C	281	10,400	Thetford p B n	29	1,100
Sempringham p G	190	7,000	Wabum p A	12	400
Sixhill p G	126	4,700	Walsingham p A	347	12,800
Spalding p B	666	24,600	Wendling a P	49	1,800
Stamford St Leonards p B	30	1,100	Westacre p A	219	8,100
Stamford St Michael p B n	33	1,200	West Dereham a P	187	6,900
Staynesfield p B n	54	2,000	Weybridge p A	4	100
Stixwold a C n	116	4,300	Wymondham a B	169	6,200
Swineshead a C	145	5,400	Creake a A not in Savine	-	-
Thornholm p A	80	3,000			
Thornton a A	532	19,600	NORTHAMPTONSHIRE		
Torksey p A	11	400	Ashby p A	77	2,900
Tupholme a P	70	2,600	Catesby p B n	106	3,900
Vaudey a C	164	6,000	Chacombe p A	53	2,000
Wellow a A	72	2,700	Fineshade p A	53	2,000
Willoughton co	142	5,300	Luffield p B	41	1,500
			N'n St Andrews p Cl	192	7,100
MIDDLESEX			N'n St James a A	132	4,900
Elsing Spital p A	211	7,800	N'n De la Pre a Cl n	76	2,800
Haliwell p B n	287	10,600	Peterborough a B	1567	57,900
Hounslow p Trin	61	2,300	Pipewell a C	264	9,700
Kilburn p B n	69	2,600	Rothwell p A n	5	200
London St Barts. p A	632	21,000	Sewardesley p C n	11	400
London Ch	553	19,000	Sulby a P	185	6,800
London St Helens p B n	329	12,100			
London Knights of St John p	1958	60,000	NORTHUMBERLAND		
St Mary Clerkenwell p B n	220	8,100	Alnwick a P	171	6,300
St Mary Graces p C	522	19,300	Bamburgh A	15	600
St Mary Bishopsgate p Bethl	477	17,600	Blanchland P	36	1,300
London Minories p Fr n	275	10,100	Brinkburne p A	62	2,300
St Thomas of Acres domus	277	10,200	Farne Island B	11	400
Stratford at Bow p B n	98	3,600	Hexham p A	111	4,100
Syon a Bridg (n)	1350	40,000	Holiscombe p B n	10	400
Westminster St Peter a B	2849	85,000	Insula Sacra p B (Lindisfarne)	22	800
			Neseham p B n	23	900
NORFOLK			Newcastle p B n	32	1,200
Beeston p A	45	1,700	Newminster a C	90	3,300
Binham p B	126	4,700	Tynemouth p B	358	13,200
Blackborough p B n	40	1,500			
Bromholm p Cl	87	3,200	NOTTINGHAMSHIRE		
Buckenham p A	97	3,600	Beauvale Ch	150	5,500
Carbroke co	63	2,300	Blyth p B	59	2,200
Carrow p B n	54	2,000	Brodholm p P	15	600
Castleacre p Cl	114	4,200	Felley p A	34	1,300
Cokesford p A	95	3,500	Lenton p Cl	147	5,400
Crabhouse p A n	23	900	Mattersey p G	35	1,300
Flitcham p A	43	1,600	Newstead in Sherwood p A	146	5,400
Hempton p A	32	1,200	Rufford a C	168	6,200
Hickling p A	84	3,100	Shelford p A	52	1,900
Horsham p B	99	3,700	Thurgarton p A	189	7,000
Hulme a B	501	18,500	Wallingwells p B n	19	700
Ingham p Trin	48	1,800	Welbeck a P	149	5,500
Langley a P	80	3,000	Worksop p A	149	5,500
Marham a C n	35	1,300			
Marmond p G	10	400	OXFORDSHIRE		
Modney p B	2	100	Bruerne a C	137	5,100
Norwich St Trinity c p B	608	22,400	Burcester p A	130	4,800
Pentney/Wormegay p A	136	5,000	Burford p ?	12	400
Shouldham p G	114	4,200	Clattercote p A	23	900
Thetford p Cl	282	10,400	Dorchester a A	75	2,800

	£s	acres
Eynsham a B	362	13,400
Godstow a B n	218	8,000
Goring p A n	33	1,200
Oseney a A	590	21,800
Rewley a C	150	5,500
Studley p B n	77	2,900
Thame a C	248	9,100
Wroxton p A	77	2,900
RUTLAND		
Brooke p A	36	1,300
SHROPSHIRE		
Bromfield p B	52	1,900
Brewood p C n	16	600
Buildwas a C	111	4,100
Chirbury p A	15	600
Haughmond a A	206	7,600
Halesowen a P	258	9,500
Lilleshall a A	210	7,700
Shrewsbury a B	374	13,800
Wenlock p Cl	312	11,500
Wombridge p A	56	2,100
SOMERSET		
Athelney a B	244	9,000
Barlinch p A	106	3,900
Bath a B	491	18,100
Bridgewater p (Fr ?)	74	2,700
Bristol St James pB	39	1,400
Bruton a A	304	11,200
Byrkley p A	5	200
Cannington p B n	48	1,800
Cleeve a C	221	8,100
Dunster p B	22	800
Glastonbury a B	2961	129,500
Hinton Ch	244	9,000
Keynsham a A	375	13,900
Minchin Bockland p A n	111	4,100
Montacute a Cl	341	12,600
Muchelney a B	355	13,100
Mynchen Barwen B n	19	700
Taunton p A	239	8,800
Templecombe co	111	4,100
Wells St John p	45	1,700
Witham Ch	216	8,000
Worspring p A	88	3,300
STAFFORDSHIRE		
Brewood p B n	245	9,000
Burton upon Trent a B	374	13,800
Croxden a C	86	3,200
Dieulacres a C	158	5,800
Dudley p Cl	14	500
Hulton a C	60	2,200
Ronton p A	50	1,900
Roucester a A	59	2,200
Stafford St Thomas p A	118	4,400
Stone p A	50	1,800
Trentham p A	76	2,800
Tutbury p B	154	5,700

	£s	acres
SUFFOLK		
Bliburgh p A	26	1,000
Brusyard a Fr n	52	1,900
Bungay p B n	32	1,200
Bury St Edmunds a B	1984	73,200
Butley p A	239	8,800
Campsey p A n	194	7,100
Eye p b	102	3,800
Flixton p A n	29	1,100
Heringfleet p A	14	500
Ipswich Holy Trinity p A	87	3,200
Ixworth p A	137	5,100
Leiston a P	151	5,600
Letheringham p A	9	300
Redlingfield pB n	62	2,300
Sibton a C	205	7,600
Sudbury p B	9	300
Wangford p Cl	17	600
Woodbridge p A	43	1,600
SURREY		
Bermondsey a B	371	13,700
Chertsey a B	532	19,600
Merton p A	683	25,200
Newark Guildford p A	197	7,300
Reigate p A	55	2,000
Shene Ch	699	25,800
St Marys Southwark p A	410	15,200
Tandridge p A	55	2,000
Waverley a C	176	6,500
SUSSEX		
Battle a B	661	24,400
Boxgrove p B	100	3,700
Dureford a P	92	3,400
Easeburn p B n	21	800
Hastings p A	41	1,500
Lewes p Cl	519	19,200
Michelham p A	140	5,200
Robertsbridge a C	228	8,400
Rusper p B n	35	1,300
Shulbrede p A	55	2,000
Tortington p A	73	2,700
WARWICKSHIRE		
Alcester p B	25	900
Avecote pB	28	1,000
Balsall co	180	6,600
Combe a C	294	10,900
Coventry p B	589	21,700
Coventry Ch	20	700
Erdbury p A	53	2,000
Henwood p B n	21	800
Kenilworth a A	338	12,500
Maxstoke p A	51	1,900
Merevale a C	205	7,600
Nuneaton p B n	211	7,800
Pinley p B n	25	900
Pollesworth a B n	54	2,000
Stonleigh a C	160	5,900
Studley p A	83	3,100

	£s	acres		£s	acres
Thelesford p Trin	19	700	Ferreby p A	71	2,600
Warwick p A	34	1,300	Fountains a C	993	32,000
Wroxall p B n	41	1,500	Gisburn p A	373	13,800
			Grosmont p B	11	400
WESTMORLAND			Haltemprice p A	95	3,500
Shap a P	93	3,400	Hampole p C n	32	1,200
			Handale p B n	18	700
WILTSHIRE	0		Helagh Park p A	65	2,400
Amesbury p B n	370	13,700	Hull Ch	157	5,800
Anstey co	73	2,700	Jervaulx a C	307	11,300
Bradenstoke p A	224	8,300	Keldholme p C n	26	1,000
Edlindon p Bon	354	13,100	Kirkham p A	242	8,900
Eston p trin	21	800	Kirklees p C n	14	500
Farleigh p Cl	145	5,400	Knaresborough p Trin	23	800
Ivychurch p A	63	2,300	Marrick p B n	50	1,800
Kington p B n	23	900	Marton p A	121	4,500
Lacock a A n	163	6,000	Meaux a C	263	9,700
Maiden Bradley p A	174	6,400	Middlesbrough p B	17	600
Malmesbury a B	764	28,200	Molesby p B n	26	1,000
Marlborough p G	32	1,200	Monk-Bretton a Cl	215	7,900
Pulton p G	18	700	Mountgrace Ch	250	9,200
Stanley a C	185	6,800	Mount St John co	73	2,700
Wilton a B n	569	21,000	Newburgh p A	180	6,600
			Newland co	109	4,000
WORCESTERSHIRE			Nostell p A	213	7,900
Bordesley a C	328	12,100	Nun Appleton C n	66	2,400
Cokehill p C n	32	1,200	Nunburnholme p B n	9	300
Dodford unknown	6	200	Nunkeeling p C n	42	1,600
Evesham a B	961	35,500	Nunmonkton B n	57	2,100
Great Malvern p B	271	10,000	Old Malton a G	177	6,500
Little Malvern p B	66	2,400	Pontefract p Cl	243	9,000
Pershore p B n	495	18,300	Ribstone co	187	6,900
Westwood p B n	59	2,200	Richmond p B	11	400
Whiston p C n	32	1,200	Rievaulx a C	250	10,000
Worcester c & p B	986	36,400	Roche a C	197	7,300
			Rosedale p B n	33	1,200
YORKSHIRE			Sawley a C	132	4,900
St Agatha's a P	150	5,500	Selby a C	500	18,400
Arden p B n	12	400	Sinningthwaite p C n	54	2,000
Arthington p B n	8	300	Swine p C n	72	2,700
Basedale p C n	20	700	Thickhed p B n	22	800
Beverley co	148	5,400	Thockwith p A	7	300
Bolton p A	180	6,600	Warter p A	129	4,800
Bridlington p A	290	10,700	Watton a G	325	12,000
Byland a C	180	6,600	Whitby a B	279	10,300
Coverham a P	105	3,900	Wickham p C n	23	900
Drax p A	56	2,100	Widkirk p A	32	1,200
Eglestone a P	49	1,800	Wilberfoss p B n	20	700
(Easby P) Ellerton p G	52	1,900	Yedlingham p B n	20	700
Elreton p C n	14	500	York St Clements a B n	38	1,400
Esholt p C n	17	600	York St Marys a B	1962	70,000

Glossary

Abbey   A monastic House controlled by an abbot (abbess) who would, in theory anyway, be chosen by his fellows with his appointment confirmed either by the secular bishop or the pope. The latter meant expensive and sometimes fruitless trips to Rome. An abbot or abbess was close to having total control over the personnel and property of the abbey.

Advowson   The right to appoint a cleric to a specific church living. Often profitable as the tithes and glebe profits could fall to the holder of the advowson who might then employ a minor curate to do the actual work of taking services for a modest stipend.

Anchorite   A hermit.

Assart   Land reclaimed from wood/waste.

Assize tenant   An occupier enjoying a rent historically fixed and often below market rates.

Boon Works   Work required by the lord (abbot) on his own land (demesne).

Bovate   The same as an Oxgang. See below.

Carucate   Alternative for Hide. See below.

Chantry   A private chapel financed for the purpose of perpetual masses for the soul(s) of the founder(s). Over 2,000 chantries had been suppressed by 1547.

Commandary   A House owned by the Knights Templar/Hospitaller and the centre for local estate management.

Copyhold tenancies   Land held by virtue of an entry in the manor court roll. Abolished in 1922.

Corrody   Board and lodging in a monastery or nunnery. Usually paid for, sometimes by a lump sum in advance – a form of annuity. Also a condition of a gift of land that the founder's kindred be fed and housed.

Croft   An enclosed area of land going with a house, often a garden and grass field.

Court of Augmentations   A government department set up by Thomas Cromwell to manage and sell the estates devolving to the Crown on the Dissolution of the monastic houses.

Customary Tenancy   Land held by custom and not at the will of the lord.

Demesne   Land held in hand 'In Manu', and not let by assize, custom, will or copyhold. In later years virtually all monastic land so held came to be let on leasehold agreements often for as long as three lives.

Farm   Before its modern meaning, land let on a lease, farmed out.

Heriot   A death duty. It came to mean the requirement that the deceased's estate should hand over the best beast or the value thereof to the lord or abbot.

Hide   Originally a unit of taxation. It came to mean the area of land which could be ploughed in a season by a team of eight oxen. It varied greatly, depending on soil type, terrain and location. It could vary between 80 and 160 acres.

Mortmain   Dead Hand. When land passed to ecclesiastical authorities, the Crown lost various revenues. This the Crown did not like and statutes were passed in 1217 and 1279 to prohibit or heavily tax such transfers.

Oxgang   Usually taken to be one eighth of a hide. The theoretical amount one ox could plough in a season.

Preceptory   The same as a Commandary.

Priory   One below an abbey in the ecclesiastical hierarchy. Headed by a prior or prioress, the appointment did not need papal authority. Many priories were richer than abbeys, could be converted to abbeys and were sometimes run in association with cathedrals.

Several   Confusingly, this meant land enclosed and no longer held in an open field or on a common.

Tenant at Will   A tenancy granted by the lord, often the Crown, which could be rescinded.

Toft   A plot of land usually with at least a garden on which a house stood or had stood.

Bibliography

'English Monasteries on the Eve of the Dissolution', Prof. A. Savine. *Oxford Studies in Social and Legal History* (1909)
The Wealth and Estates of Glastonbury Abbey at the Dissolution, Peter Clery (2003)
The Administration and Alienation of Ex-Monastic Lands by the Crown, Dr P.A. Cunich, PhD Thesis (Cambridge 1990)
Westminster Abbey and its Estates, Barbara Harvey
The Cartulary of the Knights of St John, Prof. Michael Gervers
Court of Augmentations Accounts Bedfordshire, Vols.63 and 64
Kirkstead Abbey Valor 1537, D.M. Owen (Lincs H and A Soc., Vol.24)
The Abbeys and Priories of Medieval England, Colin Platt
The Religious Orders of England, Dom David Knowles
Templars in England. Inquisition 1185, B.A. Lees
The Cistercians in Britain 1128-1540, Glyn Coppack
Estates of the Prior & Convent of Durham, (Surtees 58)
Pastoral Husbandry on a Medieval Estate, K. Biddick
Local Historian's Encyclopedia, John Richardson
Dissolution of the Monasteries, Joyce Youings
The Anglo-Saxon Chronicle, G. Garmonsway
Fountains Abbey Lease Book, D. Michelmore
Yorkshire Archeological Society Memorials
British Livestock to 1700, R. Trow Smith
Durham Priory 1400-1452, R.B. Dobson
Who's Who in Tudor England, C. Routh
Rievaulx Abbey, Fergusson and Harrison
Last Days of Henry VIII, R. Hutchinson
Monastic Britain, Ordnance Survey
Life from the Land, R. Trow Smith
Bolton Priory Rentals, I. Kershaw
English Rural Society, J.Z. Titow
Victoria County Histories
Current Ordnance Survey
Tudor England, John Guy
Valor Ecclesiasticus, 1535
National Archives

Index